THE OPTIONS PLAYBOOK™

TABLE OF CONTENTS:

WELCOME TO THE GAME

INTRODUCTION

BY BRIAN "THE OPTIONS GUY" OVERBY
TradeKing Director of Education

OPTION TRADING is a way for savvy investors to leverage assets and control some of the risks associated with playing the market. Pretty much every investor is familiar with the saying, "Buy low and sell high." But with options, it's possible to profit whether stocks are going up, down, or sideways. You can use options to cut losses, protect gains, and control large chunks of stock with a relatively small cash outlay.

On the other hand, options can be complicated and risky. Not only might you lose your entire investment, some strategies may expose you to theoretically unlimited losses.

So before you trade options, it's important to think about the effects that variables like implied volatility and time decay will have on your strategy. This playbook will help you answer those tough questions. No need to ponder, just turn to the play.

We're not going to derive the Black-Scholes option pricing model in this book. As a matter of fact, this is the only mention of the Black-Scholes model you're going to see. It's nice to know that sort of thing, but our goal was to provide the essential knowledge needed to trade a specific strategy, not to completely bore the pants off of you. After all, it's usually a good idea to wear pants while you trade. Especially if you're doing so at work.

I certainly hope you enjoy reading The Options Playbook.

Brian Overby

JUMP IN, THE WATER'S FINE

For rookies, we've created a brief overview of how options work, and outlined some plays to help you get started. These strategies will help familiarize you with the option market without leaving your proverbial backside overexposed to risk.

Don't get us wrong, however. All option trades involve risk and are not suited to all investors. Option contracts usually represent 100 shares of stock, so be careful. You should avoid trading more options than the number of shares you're used to.

If you typically trade 100 shares of stock, trade one option contract. If you typically trade 200 shares, trade two option contracts, and so on. (Get used to hearing us say that last bit. We'll be repeating it often, and for good reason.)

STAY MENTALLY TOUGH OUT THERE

For more experienced option traders, we hope this playbook will serve as a convenient reference tool. Here, you'll find the construction and risk profiles for many different strategies. That means you can stay focused on forecasting or analyzing "The Greeks," instead of experiencing brain strain while trying to remember exactly how to set up a long iron condor.

For each play, we've pointed out key indicators to look for using the option tools on TradeKing.com. These tools can be an invaluable resource for option traders. So remember to use them as much as possible. (Tattooing our URL on the back of your hand might help in this regard.)

We'll be honest, you're not going to reap windfall profits every time. So don't dig fingernail marks into your desk or tear out clumps of your hair every time you're about to get hit with a loss. Sometimes you make money and sometimes you lose money. It's all part of the game. The idea is simply to run the right plays, and win more often than you lose.

LET'S GET BUSY

We're not going to overload you with minute details about how the option market works, how options are priced, and that kind of thing. There are already plenty of textbooks out there designed to do that. This playbook is simply a breakdown of the most common option plays.

If you're still hungry for knowledge when you get to the end, head to TradeKing.com and visit our learning center. There's plenty there to satisfy even the most gargantuan mind.

Options are a great topic for cocktail party chitchat.

GOOD PLACES TO STUDY THIS PLAYBOOK

- IN AN AIRPLANE
- IN A CAR (AS LONG AS YOU'RE NOT DRIVING)
- BY THE POOL
- ON THE CAN
- IN BED
- IN A WAITING ROOM
- AT WORK
- ON THE TRAIN
- AT YOUR COMPUTER WHILE TRADING ON TRADEKING.COM
- WHILE SIPPING A COCKTAIL

BAD PLACE TO STUDY THIS PLAYBOOK

• ON A TRAMPOLINE

THE LONG AND SHORT OF THINGS

TAKING STOCK OF THE SITUATION

HERE are a few things you absolutely need to understand before this playbook will make as much sense to you as we hope it will. Some of you probably already know these terms and concepts. Or at least think you do. But how will you really know you know them unless you read this section? Therein lies the paradox.

Of course, if you're a seasoned veteran or MVP, by all means skip right ahead to the plays. And for you Rookies, well, read on. We'll keep it interesting.

THROUGHOUT THIS BOOK we talk about the "stock" that options are based on. That's a bit of an oversimplification. Actually, options can be traded on several kinds of underlying securities. Some of the most common ones are stocks, indexes, or ETFs (Exchange Traded Funds). So feel free to substitute these terms to match your preferred style of trading.

WHAT'S AN OPTION?

OPTIONS ARE CONTRACTS giving the owner the right to buy or sell an asset at a fixed price (called the "strike price") for a specific period of time. That period of time could be as short as a day or as long as a couple of years, depending on the option. The seller of the option contract has to take the opposite side of the trade if and when the owner exercises the right to buy or sell the asset.

Here's an example of a standard quote on an option.

That's the stock that the option is based on. Not an indication your fly is down. It usually represents 100 shares.

That's the "strike price" for the stock. So the stock will change hands at $70 if the option is exercised.

That's the "premium," or per-share cost of the option. Option contracts usually represent 100 shares of the underlying stock, so you'll actually pay $310 plus commission for this contract. ($3.10 x 100 = $310)

XYZ JANUARY 70 CALL AT $3.10

That's the month the option expires. The last day to trade the option is usually the third Friday of this month.

That's the type of option. There are two kinds of options: calls and puts. They're defined later.

DEFINITIONS

Don't worry if some of these meanings aren't crystal clear at first. That's normal. Just keep forging ahead, and everything will become more apparent over time.

LONG – This term can be pretty confusing. In this book, it usually doesn't refer to time. As in "TradeKing never leaves me on hold for long." Or distance, as in "I went for a long jog."

When you're talking about options and stocks, "long" implies a position of ownership. After you have purchased an option or a stock, you are considered to be long that security in your account.

SHORT – Short is another one of those words you have to be careful about. It doesn't refer to your hair after a buzz cut, or that time at camp when you short-sheeted your counselor's bed.

If you've sold an option or a stock without actually owning it, you are then considered to be "short" that security in your account. That's one of the interesting things about options. You can sell something that you don't actually own. But when you do, you may be obligated to do something at a later date. As you read through this book, you'll get a clearer picture of what that "something" might be for specific plays.

CALL OPTIONS (OFTEN SHORTENED TO "CALL") – When you buy a call option, you have the right (but not the obligation) to purchase a specific security at a specific price within a specific time frame. A good way to remember this: You have the right to "call" stock away from somebody.

(If, however, you're considering phoning your ex-lover after a few cocktails, "call option" means something else entirely. We recommend you steer clear of that one.)

PUT OPTIONS (OFTEN SHORTENED TO "PUT") – When you buy a put option, you have the right (but not the obligation) to sell a specific security at a specific price within a specific time frame. A good way to remember this: You have the right to "put" stock to somebody.

STRIKE PRICE – The pre-agreed price per share at which stock may be bought or sold under the terms of an option contract. We've mentioned Strike Price a couple of times already, but we just want to make sure we hammer the definition home. Some people refer to the strike price as the "exercise price."

IN-THE-MONEY (ITM) – For call options, this means the stock price is above the strike price. So if a call has a strike price of $50 and the stock is trading at $55, that option is in-the-money.

For put options, it means the stock price is below the strike price. So if a put has a strike price of $50 and the stock is trading at $45, that option is in-the-money.

This term might also remind you of a great song from the 1930s that you can tap dance to whenever your option plays go according to plan.

OUT-OF-THE-MONEY (OTM) – For call options, this means the stock price is below the strike price. For put options, this means the stock price is above the strike price. The cost of out-of-the-money options consists entirely of "time value."

AT-THE-MONEY (ATM) – An option is "at-the-money" when the stock price is equal to the strike price. (Since the two values are rarely exactly equal, when purchasing options the strike price closest to the stock price is typically called the 'ATM strike.')

INTRINSIC VALUE – The amount an option is in-the-money. Obviously, only in-the-money options have intrinsic value.

TIME VALUE – The part of an option price that is based on its time to expiration. If you subtract the amount of intrinsic value from an option price, you're left with the time value. If an option has no intrinsic value (i.e., it's out-of-the-money) its entire worth is based on time value.

We would also like to take this opportunity to say while you're reading this book you're spending your time valuably.

EXERCISE – This occurs when the owner of an option invokes the right embedded in the option contract. In layman's terms, it means the option owner buys or sells the underlying stock at the strike price, and requires the option seller to take the other side of the trade.

Interestingly, options are a lot like most people, in that exercise is a fairly infrequent event. (See "Cashing Out Your Options," on p.16.)

ASSIGNMENT – When an option owner exercises the option, an option seller (or "writer") is assigned and must make good on his or her obligation. That means they are required to buy or sell the underlying stock at the strike price.

NOTE: For purposes of this book, "assignment" has nothing to do with those recurring dreams most people have about being back in school and forgetting to do their homework assignments. It may, however, involve recurring dreams about not closing an option before expiration. More on that later.

INDEX OPTIONS VS. EQUITY OPTIONS – In this book, we occasionally make reference to index options. There are a few differences between index options and equity options, and it's important for you to understand them. First, index options typically can't be exercised prior to expiration, whereas equity options typically can. Second, the last day to trade most index options is the Thursday before the third Friday of the expiration month, whereas the last day to trade equity options is the third Friday of the expiration month. Third, index options are cash-settled, but equity options result in stock changing hands.

NOTE: There are several exceptions to these general guidelines about index options. If you're going to trade an index, you must take the time to understand its characteristics. To find out more, visit cboe.com or ask a TradeKing broker.

STANDARD DEVIATION – This is a book about options, not statistics. But we use this term a lot, so we should clarify it a little. If we assume stocks have a simple normal price distribution, we can calculate what a one standard deviation move for the stock will be.

If you multiply the stock price by the implied volatility, that will give you a one standard deviation move over a one-year period. On an annualized basis the stock will stay within plus or minus one standard deviation roughly 68% of the time. The concept is, if you take one bazillion stocks that are trading at $50 with 25% implied volatility, the one standard deviation move is $12.50. So one year from now around 68% of them should be within a range of $37.50-$62.50.

NOTE: For simplicity, here we assume a normal distribution. Most pricing models assume a log-normal distribution. Just in case you're a Statistician or something.

WHAT IS VOLATILITY?

As an individual retail trader you really only need to worry about two forms of volatility: historic volatility and implied volatility. (Unless your temper is particularly volatile, in which case you should probably worry about that, too.)

HISTORIC VOLATILITY is defined in textbooks as the annualized standard deviation of past stock price movements. But since this isn't a textbook and we don't want to bore you silly, we'll just say it's how much the stock price fluctuated in a one-year period.

IMPLIED VOLATILITY is what the marketplace is "implying" the volatility of the stock will be in the future, without regard for direction. Based on truth and rumors in the marketplace, the prices of certain options will begin to change.

If there's an earnings announcement or a major court decision coming up, traders will alter trading patterns on certain options. That drives the price of the options up or down, independent of the stock price movement. The implied volatility is derived from the cost of those options. So if there were no options traded on the stock, there would be no way to calculate the implied volatility.

Ultimately, implied volatility can help you gauge how much the marketplace thinks the stock price might swing in the future. More specifically, it enables you to calculate a one standard deviation move for the stock. For example, if you have a stock trading at $100 with an implied volatility of 20%, the one standard deviation move is plus or minus $20. (20% of $100 equals $20.) That means at the end of one year there's a 68% chance it will end up somewhere between $80 and $120. (See an example at right.)

Remember, implied volatility is just a forecast, not an exact predictor of stock movement. After all, it's not as if Nostradamus works down on the trading floor.

We could go on and on about normal distribution, log-normal distribution and the expected range of the underlying stock. But then your eyes might start to glaze over.

So for the purposes of this playbook, let's just say when implied volatility increases, the price of options will usually increase. That's because it's implying a wider potential range of movement on the underlying stock. So increasing implied volatility is good for the option buyer and bad for the option seller.

Conversely, if implied volatility decreases, the price of options will usually decrease because it's implying a smaller potential range of movement on the underlying stock. That's good for the option seller and bad for the option buyer.

NORMAL DISTRIBUTION OF STOCK PRICE

Stock = **$100**
Implied Volatility = **20%**

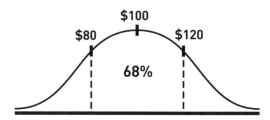

In theory, there's a 68% probability that a stock trading at $100 with an implied volatility of 20% will cost between $80 and $120 a year later. But remember, the operative words are "in theory," since implied volatility isn't an exact science.

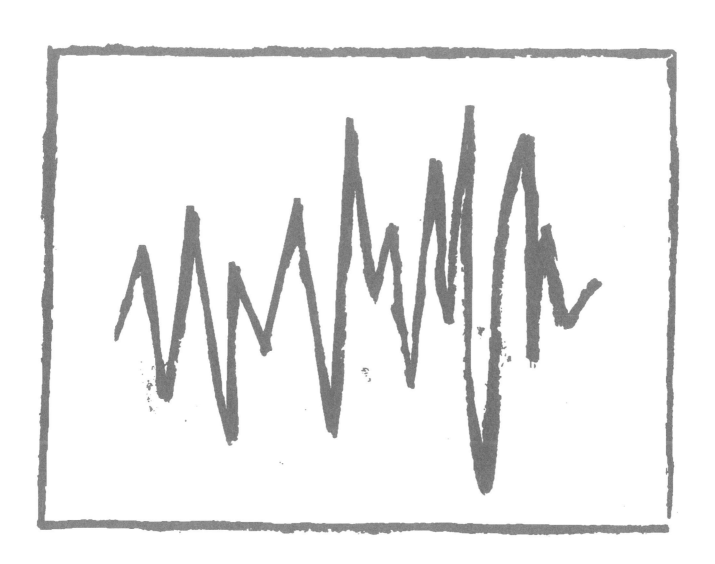

MEET THE GREEKS

(AT LEAST THE THREE MOST IMPORTANT ONES)

Before you read the plays, it's a good idea to get to know these characters since they'll help you decipher how your options react to changes in the marketplace. Keep in mind as you're getting acquainted, the examples we use are "ideal world" examples. And as Plato would certainly tell you, in the real world things tend not to work quite as perfectly as they do in an ideal one.

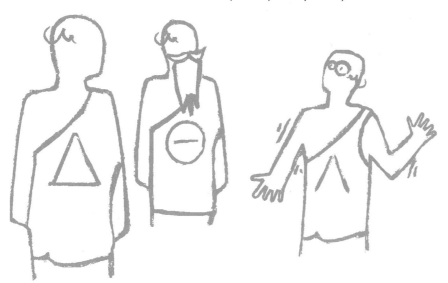

DELTA

Beginning options traders sometimes assume that when a stock moves $1, the cost of all options based on it will also move $1. That's pretty silly when you really think about it. The option costs much less than the stock. Why should you reap the same benefits as if you owned the stock? So the real question is, how much will the price of an option move if the stock moves $1? That's where delta comes in.

"Delta" is the amount an option will move based on a dollar change in the underlying stock.

Calls have positive delta (between 0 and 1). That means if the stock goes up, the price for the call will go up. Here's an example: If a call has a delta of .50 and the stock goes up $1.00, in theory, the price of the call will go up about 50 cents. If the stock goes down $1.00, in theory, the price of the call will go down about 50 cents.

Out-of-the-money options will move less than in-the-money options. So as expiration approaches, the delta for "in-the-money" calls will approach 1. Delta for "out-of-the-money" calls will approach 0. That's because the options will either be exercised and "become stock," or they will expire worthless and become nothing at all.

Puts have a negative delta (between 0 and -1). That means if the stock goes up, the price of the option will go down. For example, if a put has a delta of -.50 and the stock goes up $1.00, in theory, the price of the put will go down

NOTE: The Greeks represent the consensus of the marketplace as to the how the option will react to changes in certain variables associated with the pricing of an option contract. There is no guarantee that these forecasts will be correct.

50 cents. If the stock goes down $1.00, in theory, the price of the put will go up 50 cents. Out-of-the-money options will move less than in-the-money options. So as expiration approaches, the delta for "in-the-money" puts will approach -1. Delta for "out-of-the-money" puts will approach 0.

THETA

Theta, or "time decay," is enemy number one for the option buyer. On the other hand, it's usually the option seller's best friend. It's the amount an option's price will change (at least in theory) for a one-day change in the time to expiration. In the options market, the passage of time is similar to the effect of the hot summer sun on a block of ice. Each hour that passes causes some of the option's value to "melt away." Furthermore, not only does the time premium melt away, but it does so at an accelerated rate as expiration approaches.

When reading the plays, watch for the effects of theta in the section called "As Time Goes By."

VEGA

You can think of vega as the Greek who's a little unstable. It's the amount an option's price will change in theory for a corresponding one-point change in the implied volatility of the option contract. Keep in mind, vega does not have any effect on the intrinsic value of options; it only affects the "time value" of the option's price.

When reading the plays, watch for the effects of vega in the section called "Implied Volatility."

NOTE: Vega is not actually a Greek letter. But since it starts with a 'V' and measures changes in volatility, the name stuck.

WHERE ARE GAMMA AND RHO?

You might have noticed we're missing a couple of Greeks here. Namely, gamma and rho. Don't mind them. They just stepped out for a gyro, since we don't talk about them that much in this book.

Here's an indication of what these other two Greeks are usually up to. Those of you who really get serious about options will eventually get to know them far more intimately.

GAMMA is the rate that delta changes based on a $1 change in the stock price. You can think of gamma as "acceleration" in the rate at which option values change.

RHO is the amount an option value changes based on a 1% change in interest rates.

CASHING OUT YOUR OPTIONS

So, you've bought or sold options to open a "long" or "short" position. What now? There are three possible results of your trade.

1) The options are bought or sold to "close" the position prior to expiration.

2) The options expire worthless.

3) The options are exercised or assigned prior to or at expiration, resulting in a trade of the underlying stock.

There's a common misconception that #2 is the most frequent result. Not so. Outcome #1 is the most frequent. That's why it makes so much sense that we listed it #1.

If you have an option trade that's working in your favor, you can cash in. If you have a trade that's going against you, it's OK to cut and run. In the options world, that means closing out and moving on to the next trade.

You don't necessarily have to wait until expiration to "see what happens." Oftentimes the way to go is to close your position before your option contract(s) expire.

Options aren't necessarily a hot potato that gets passed around and winds up in someone's hands at expiration. Once an option is closed in the marketplace, it ceases to exist. That's why when you enter an order, it says buy or sell "to open" or "to close." The Options Clearing Corporation keeps track of that sort of thing.

OPTION OUTCOMES*

Source: Options Clearing Corporation
* Calendar year 2006

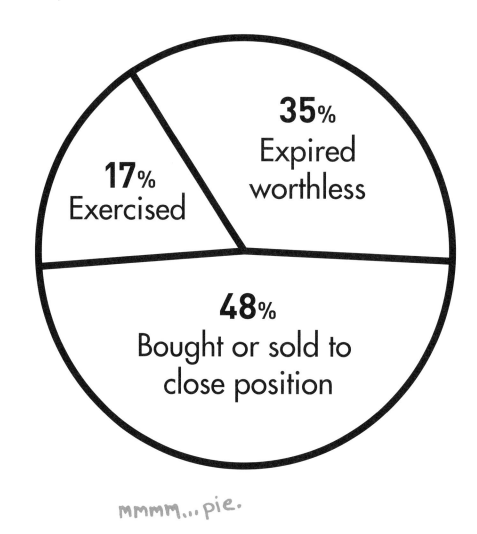

35% Expired worthless

17% Exercised

48% Bought or sold to close position

mmmm...pie.

AND NOW, FOR A QUICK DISCLAIMER

Commissions are a very important part of options trading and they can impact your bottom line. However, to make this book easy to read, we don't talk about them very much.

At any rate, TradeKing's commissions are among the lowest in the business. So don't worry. We won't nickel and dime you. If we wanted to engage in chiseling, we would have become sculptors instead of brokers.

Just remember to factor the cost of each trade into your profit and loss calculations.

ROOKIE'S

CORNER

GETTING
YOUR FEET WET
WITHOUT GETTING IN
UP TO YOUR
YOU-KNOW-WHAT

Option trading is more complicated than trading stock. And for a first-timer, it can be a little intimidating. That's why many investors decide to begin trading options by buying short-term calls. Especially "out-of-the-money" calls (strike price above the stock price), since they seem to follow a familiar pattern: Buy low, sell high.

But for most investors, buying out-of-the-money short-term calls are probably not the best way to start trading options. Let's look at an example of why this is the case.

Imagine you're bullish on stock XYZ, trading at $50. As a beginning option trader, you might be tempted to buy calls 30 days from expiration with a strike price of $55, at a cost of $0.15, or $15 per contract. Why? Because you can buy a lot of them. Let's do the math. (And remember, one option contract usually equals 100 shares.)

Purchasing 100 shares of XYZ at $50 would cost $5000. But for the same $5000, you could buy 333 contracts of $55 calls, and control 33,300 shares. Holy smokes.

Imagine XYZ hits $56 within the next 30 days, and the $55 call trades at $1.05 just prior to expiration. You'd make $29,970 in a month ($34,965 sale price minus $4995 initially paid) less commissions. At first glance, that kind of leverage is very attractive indeed.

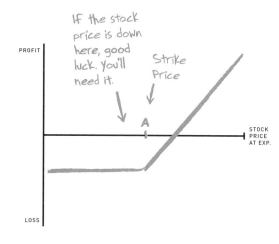

CALL OPTION RISK PROFILE

When you buy a call option with a strike price of $55 at a cost of $0.15, and the stock currently trading at $50, you need the stock price to rise $5.15 before your options expire in order to break even. That's a pretty significant rise in a short time. And that kind of move can be very difficult to predict.

ALL THAT GLITTERS ISN'T A GOLDEN OPTIONS TRADE

One of the problems with short-term out-of-the-money calls is that you not only have to be right about the direction the stock moves, but you also have to be right about the timing. That ratchets up the degree of difficulty.

Furthermore, to make a profit, the stock doesn't merely need to go past the strike price within a predetermined period of time. It needs to go past the strike price plus the cost of the option. In the case of the $55 call on stock XYZ, you'd need the stock to reach $55.15 within 30 days just to break even. And that doesn't even factor in commissions.

In essence, you're asking the stock to move more than 10% in less than a month. How many stocks are likely to do that? The answer you're looking for is, "Not many." In all probability, the stock won't reach the strike price, and the options will expire worthless. So in order to make money on an out-of-the-money call, you either need to outwit the market, or get plain lucky.

BEING CLOSE MEANS NO CIGAR

Imagine the stock rose to $54 during the 30 days of your option's lifetime. You were right about the direction the stock moved. But since you were wrong about how far it would go within a specific time frame, you'd lose your entire investment.

If you'd simply bought 100 shares of XYZ at $50, you'd be up $400. Even if your forecast was wrong and XYZ went down in price, it would most likely still be worth a significant portion of your initial investment. So the moral of the story is:

Don't get suckered in by the leverage you get from buying boatloads of short-term out-of-the-money calls.

HEY, DON'T GET US WRONG

On the other hand, don't get the false impression that you should avoid calls altogether. In this book, we've outlined several ways to approach using them. In fact, this section outlines three plays for beginners to get their feet wet, and two of them do involve calls.

These plays are: A) writing covered calls, B) buying LEAPS® calls (long-term options) as a stock substitute, and C) selling puts on a stock you want to buy.

The reason we chose these plays is because they're designed to enhance your stock portfolio. For now, rookies should aim for a balance between trading stocks and using options when you feel it's appropriate.

LEAPS is a registered trademark of CBOE

WRITING COVERED CALLS

Writing a covered call means you're selling someone else the right to purchase a stock that you already own, at a specific price, within a specified time frame. Because one option contract represents 100 shares, to run this play, you must own at least 100 shares for every call contract you sell.

As a result of selling ("writing") the call, you'll pocket the premium right off the bat. The fact that you already own the stock means you're "covered" if the stock price rises past the strike price and the call options are "assigned." You'll simply deliver stock you already own, reaping the additional benefit of the uptick on the stock.

HERE'S HOW YOU CAN WRITE YOUR FIRST COVERED CALL

First, choose a stock in your portfolio that has already performed fairly well, and which you are willing to sell if the call option is assigned. Avoid choosing a stock that you're very bullish on in the long-term. That way you won't feel too heartbroken if you do have to part with the stock and wind up missing out on further gains.

Now pick a strike price at which you'd be comfortable selling the stock. Normally, the strike price you choose should be out-of-the-money. That's because the goal is for the stock to rise further in price before you'll have to part with it.

Next, pick an expiration date for the option contract. Consider 30-45 days in the future as a starting point, but use your judgment. You want to look for a date that provides an acceptable premium for selling the call option at your chosen strike price.

As a general rule of thumb, some investors think about 2% of the stock value is an acceptable premium to look for. Remember, with options, time is money. The further you go out in time, the more an option will be worth. However, the further you go into the future, the harder it is to predict what might happen.

On the other hand, beware of receiving too much time premium. If the premium seems abnormally high, there's usually a reason for it. Check for news in the marketplace that may affect the price of the stock, and remember if something seems too good to be true, it usually is.

Here's a helpful hint: Try using the covered call chain on TradeKing.com to determine your optimal strike price and expiration date for the calls you plan to sell.

There are three possible outcomes:

SCENARIO 1: THE STOCK GOES DOWN

If the stock price is down at the time the option expires, the good news is the call will expire worthless, and you'll keep the entire premium received for selling it. Obviously, the bad news is that the value of the stock is down. That's the nature of a covered call. The risk comes from owning the stock. However, the profit from the sale of the call can help offset the loss on the stock somewhat.

If the stock takes a dive prior to the expiration date of the call, don't panic. You're not locked into your position. Although losses will be accruing on the stock, the call option you sold will go down in value as well. It's possible to buy the call back for less money than you received to sell it. If your opinion on the stock has changed, you can simply close your position by buying back the call contract, and then dump the stock.

SCENARIO 2: THE STOCK STAYS THE SAME OR GOES UP A LITTLE, BUT DOESN'T REACH THE STRIKE PRICE

There's really no bad news in this scenario. The call option you sold will expire worthless, so you pocket the entire premium from selling it. Perhaps you've seen some gains on the underlying stock, which you will still own. You can't complain about that.

SCENARIO 3: THE STOCK RISES ABOVE THE STRIKE PRICE

If the stock is above the strike price at expiration, the call option will be assigned and you'll have to sell 100 shares of the stock.

If the stock skyrockets after you sell the shares, you might consider kicking yourself for missing out on any additional gains, but don't. You made a conscious decision that you were willing to part with the stock at the strike price, and you achieved the maximum profit potential from the play.

Pat yourself on the back. Or if you're not very flexible, have somebody else pat your back for you. You've done well.

THE RECAP ON THE LOGIC

Many investors use a covered call as a first foray into option trading. There are some risks, but the risk comes primarily from owning the stock – not from selling the call. The sale of the option only limits opportunity on the upside.

When running a covered call, you're taking advantage of "time decay" on the options you sold. Every day the stock doesn't move, the call you sold will decline in value, which benefits you as the seller. (Time decay is an important concept. So as a beginner, it's good for you to see it in action.)

As long as the stock price doesn't reach the strike price, your stock won't get called away. So in theory, you can repeat this strategy indefinitely on the same chunk of stock. And with every covered call you run, you'll become more familiar with the workings of the option market.

You may also appear smarter to yourself when you look in the mirror. But we're not making any promises about that.

this can be painful

usually painless (unless there is sunburn involved)

BUYING LEAPS® CALLS AS A STOCK SUBSTITUTE

We've already warned you against starting off by purchasing out-of-the-money short-term calls. Here's a method of using calls that might work for the beginning option trader: buying long-term calls, or "LEAPS."

The goal here is to reap benefits similar to those you'd see if you owned the stock, while limiting the risks you'd face by having the stock in your portfolio. In effect, your LEAPS call acts as a "stock substitute."

WHAT ARE "LEAPS?"

LEAPS are longer-term options. The term stands for "Long-term Equity AnticiPation Securities," in case you're the kind of person who wonders about that sort of thing. And no, that capital P in AnticiPation wasn't a typo, in case you're the kind of person who wonders about that sort of thing too.

Options with more than 9 months until expiration are considered LEAPS. They behave just like other options, so don't let the term confuse you. It simply means that they have a long "shelf-life."

LET'S GET STARTED

First, choose a stock. You should use exactly the same process you would use if purchasing the stock. Go to TradeKing's Quotes + Research menu, and analyze the stock's fundamentals to make sure you like it.

Now, you need to pick your strike price. You want to buy a LEAPS call that is deep in-the-money. (When talking about a call, "in-the-money" means the strike price is below the current stock price.) A general rule of thumb to use while running this play is to look for a delta of .80 or more at the strike price you choose.

Remember, a delta of .80 means that if the stock rises $1, then in theory, the price of your option will rise $0.80. If delta is .90, then if the stock rises $1, in theory your options will rise $0.90, and so forth. The delta at each strike price will be displayed on TradeKing's option chains.

As a starting point, consider a LEAPS call that is at least 20% of the stock price in-the-money. (For example, if the underlying stock costs $100, buy a call with a strike price of $80 or lower.) However, for particularly volatile stocks, you may need to go deeper in-the-money to get the delta you're looking for.

The deeper in-the-money you go, the more expensive your option will be. That's because it will have more "intrinsic value." But the benefit is that it will also have a higher delta. And the higher your delta, the more your option will behave as a stock substitute.

THE CAVEAT

You must keep in mind that even long-term options have an expiration date. If the stock shoots skyward the day after your option expires, it does you no good. Furthermore, as expiration approaches, options lose their value at an accelerating rate. So pick your time frame carefully.

As a general rule of thumb, consider buying a call that won't expire for at least a year or more. That makes this play a fine strategy for the longer-term investor. After all, we are treating this strategy as an investment, not pure speculation.

PICK A NUMBER

Now that you've chosen your strike price and month of expiration, you need to decide how many LEAPS calls to buy. As we say so many times in this book, you should usually trade the same quantity of options as the number of shares you're accustomed to trading. Pardon us for being redundant, but that's important.

If you'd typically buy 100 shares, buy one call. If you'd typically buy 200 shares, buy two calls, and so on. Don't go too crazy, because if your call options finish out-of-the-money, you may lose your entire investment.

HURRY UP AND WAIT

Now that you've purchased your LEAPS call(s), it's time to play the waiting game. Just like when you're trading stocks, you need to have a predefined price at which you'll be satisfied with your option gains, and get out of your position. You also need a pre-defined stop-loss if the price of your option(s) go down sharply.

Trading psychology is a big part of being a successful option investor. Be consistent. Stick to your guns. Don't panic. And don't get too greedy.

SELLING CASH-SECURED PUTS ON STOCK YOU WANT TO BUY

What if you could buy stocks lower than the current market price? And what if you could make money when you're wrong about the direction of the market? If either of those scenarios sounds appealing to you, then perhaps you should consider selling a cash-secured put.

WHEN TO RUN THIS PLAY

You're long-term bullish on a stock, but you don't want to pay the current market price for it. In other words, if the stock dips, you wouldn't mind buying it. You might consider entering a limit order at the price you'd like to pay for the shares. But selling a cash-secured put gives you another method of buying the stock below the current market price, with the added benefit of receiving the premium from the sale of the put.

HOW TO DO IT

Sell an out-of-the-money put (strike price below the stock price). You may want to consider choosing the first strike price below the current trading price for the stock, because that will increase the probability the put will be assigned, and you'll wind up acquiring the stock.

In order to receive a desirable premium, a time frame to shoot for when selling the put is anywhere from 30-45 days from expiration. This will enable you to take advantage of accelerating "time decay" on the option's price as expiration approaches and hopefully provide enough premium to be worth your while. But what you consider a good return is up to you.

Once you've chosen your strike price and month of expiration, you'll need to make sure there's enough cash in your account to pay for the shares if the put is assigned (hence the term "cash-secured" puts).

Ideally, you want the stock price to dip slightly below the strike price, and stay there until expiration. That way, the buyer of your put will exercise it, you will be assigned, and you'll be obligated to buy the stock. The premium received from selling the put can be applied to the cost of the shares, ultimately lowering the cost basis of the stock purchase.

LET'S LOOK AT SOME EXAMPLES OF WHAT MIGHT HAPPEN

Imagine stock XYZ is trading at $52 per share, but you want to pay less than $50 per share for 100 shares. You sell one put contract with a strike price of $50, 45 days prior to expiration, and receive a premium of $1. Since one contract usually equals 100 shares, you receive a total of $100.

If the put is assigned, you'll be obligated to buy 100 shares of XYZ at $50. In order to be cash-secured, you'll need at least $5000 in your account. Since you've already received $100 from the sale of the put, you only need to come up with the additional $4900.

How might this trade pan out? Let's examine four possible outcomes.

SCENARIO 1: THE STOCK DIPS SLIGHTLY BELOW $50

This is a great scenario. Let's say the stock is at $49.75 at expiration. The put will be assigned, and you will buy 100 shares at $50 per share. However, since you already received a $1 per share premium for the sale of the put, it's as if you paid net $49 per share. Since the stock is currently trading for $49.75, you achieved a savings of $75 ($0.75 x 100 shares). Huzzah.

SCENARIO 2: THE STOCK RISES

Now imagine the stock rises, and ends up at $54 at expiration. That means there's some bad news, but there's some good news too. The bad news is you were wrong about the short-term movement of the stock. Since it didn't come down to the strike price, the put won't be assigned and you won't get the stock at $50 per share. If you had simply bought the stock at $52 instead of selling the put, you would have already made $2 per share: double the $1 premium you received.

On the other hand, you did receive a $1 premium, or $100 total for being wrong. And there's nothing wrong with that. Plus, the cash you used to secure your put will be available to you for other trades. So there's a silver lining to this otherwise cloudy trade.

SCENARIO 3: THE STOCK DIPS SLIGHTLY FURTHER THAN YOU ANTICIPATED

What if the stock is at $48 as the options expire? The put will be assigned and you will pay $50 per share. Subtracting the $1 put premium received, it is as if you paid $49 per share. You may be tempted to curse and think you overpaid for the stock by $1 per share.

But look at the bright side. If you hadn't used this strategy, you might've simply entered a limit order at $50 and not even received the put premium. That would be worse, right? Plus, now that you own the stock, it might make a rebound. Let's hope you're a good long-term stock picker.

SCENARIO 4: THE STOCK COMPLETELY TANKS

This is obviously the worst-case scenario. Let's hope your forecasting would never be this wrong. But what if the stock does completely tank? There are a couple of things you can do.

First, you can accept assignment and pay $50 per share, irrespective of current stock price. In this case, you'd be hoping your long-term forecast is correct, and the stock will bounce back significantly.

If you doubt the stock will make a recovery, your other choice is to close your position prior to expiration. That will remove any obligation you have to buy the stock. To close your position, simply buy back the 50-Strike put. Keep in mind, the further the stock price goes down, the more expensive that will be.

This scenario demonstrates the importance of having a stop-loss plan in place. If the stock goes beneath the lowest point where you're comfortable buying it, a stop order should be placed to buy back the 50-Strike put. This is much the same concept as a stop order you might have on stocks in your portfolio.

THE RECAP ON THE LOGIC

Selling cash-secured puts is a substitute for placing a limit order on a stock you wish to own. You receive a premium for selling the puts, and if the options are assigned, the premium can be applied to the purchase of the stock.

If the stock doesn't dip below the strike price by expiration, the puts will probably not be assigned, and you won't have the opportunity to buy the stock at the strike price. However, the options will expire worthless and you'll get to keep the premium. And that's a good thing.

Just remember, only sell puts on the number of shares you can reasonably afford to buy. And have a stop-loss plan in place, in case the stock goes completely in the tank.

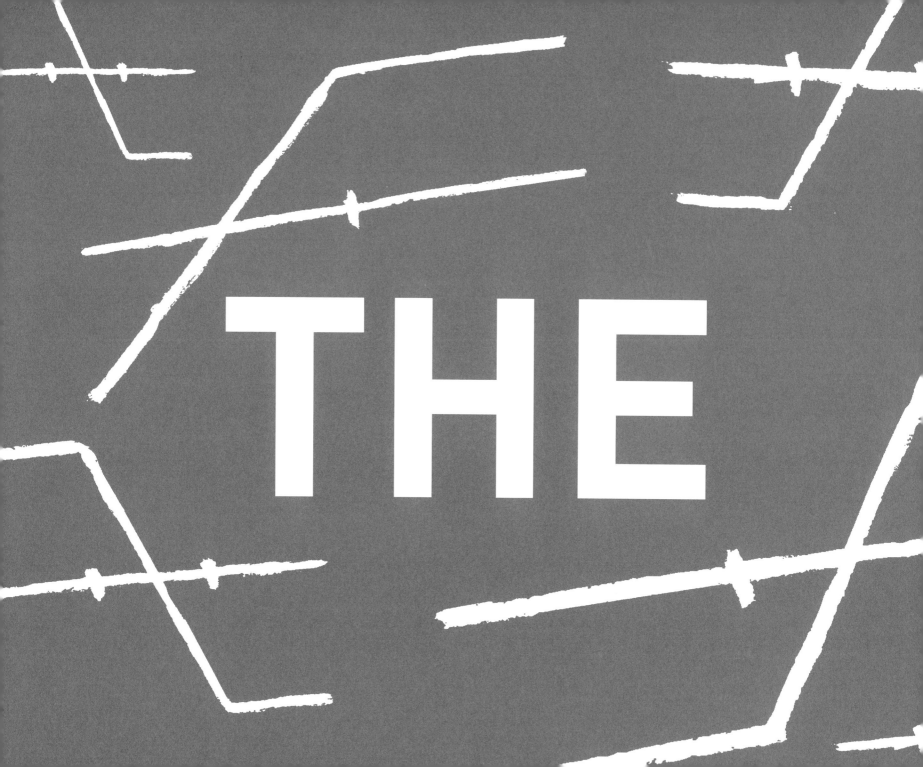

WHERE TO FIND YOUR FAVORITE PLAYS

KEY TO INTERPRETING SYMBOLS

⬤ ›› BULLISH

⬤ ›› BEARISH

Ⓝ ›› NEUTRAL

❓ ›› NOT SURE - You think the stock is going someplace, but you don't know which direction.

LONG CALL

THE SETUP

- Buy a call, Strike Price A

- Generally, the stock price will be at or above Strike A

WHO SHOULD RUN IT

Veterans and higher

NOTE: Many rookies begin trading options by purchasing out-of-the-money short-term calls. That's because they tend to be cheap, and you can buy a lot of them. However, they're probably not the best way to get your feet wet. See the "Rookie's Corner" section of this book for other plays to consider.

WHEN TO RUN IT

 You're bullish as a matador.

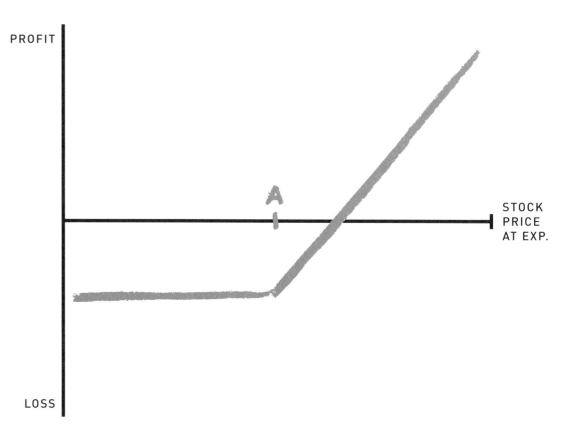

THE STRATEGY

A long call gives you the right to buy the underlying stock at Strike Price A.

Calls may be used as an alternative to buying stock outright. You can profit if the stock rises, while limiting the risk that could result from purchasing the stock. It is also possible to gain leverage over a greater number of shares because calls are usually considerably less expensive than the stock itself.

But be careful, especially with short-term out-of-the-money calls. If you buy too many option contracts, you are actually increasing your risk. Options may expire worthless and you can lose your entire investment, whereas if you own the stock it will usually still be worth something. (Except for certain energy stocks that shall remain nameless.)

OPTIONS GUY'S TIPS:

☞ Don't go overboard with the leverage you can get when buying calls. A general rule of thumb is this: If you're used to buying 100 shares of stock per trade, buy one option contract (1 contract = 100 shares). If you're comfortable buying 200 shares, buy two option contracts, and so on.

☞ If you do purchase a call, you may wish to consider buying the contract in-the-money, since it's likely to have a larger delta (that is, changes in the option's value will correspond more closely with any change in the stock price). Try looking for a delta of .80 or greater if possible. In-the-money options are more expensive because they have intrinsic value, but you get what you pay for.

BREAK-EVEN AT EXPIRATION

Strike A plus the cost of the call.

THE SWEET SPOT

The stock goes through the roof.

MAXIMUM POTENTIAL PROFIT

There's a theoretically unlimited profit potential, if the stock goes to infinity. (Please note: We've never seen a stock go to infinity. Sorry.)

MAXIMUM POTENTIAL LOSS

Risk is limited to the premium paid for the call option.

MARGIN REQUIREMENT

After the trade is paid for, no additional margin is required.

AS TIME GOES BY

For this play, time decay is the enemy. It will negatively affect the value of the option you bought.

IMPLIED VOLATILITY

After the play is established, increasing implied volatility is your friend. It will increase the value of the option you bought. It also reflects an increased possibility of a price swing (without regard for direction).

CHECK YOUR PLAY WITH TRADEKING TOOLS

• Use the Profit + Loss Calculator to establish break-even points, evaluate how your strategy might change as expiration approaches, and analyze the Greeks.

• Remember: If options are cheap, they're usually cheap for a reason. Use the Probability Calculator to help you form an opinion on your option's chances of expiring in-the-money.

• Use the Technical Analysis Tool to look for bullish indicators.

LONG PUT

THE SETUP

• Buy a put, Strike Price A

• Generally, the stock price will be at or below Strike A

WHO SHOULD RUN IT

Veterans and higher

WHEN TO RUN IT

 You're bearish as a grizzly.

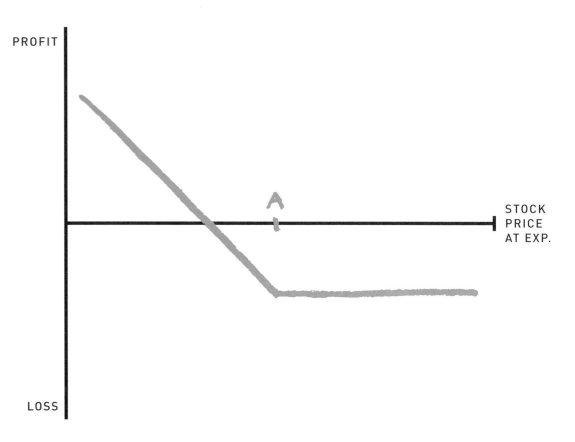

THE STRATEGY

A long put gives you the right to sell the underlying stock at Strike Price A.

If there were no such thing as puts, the only way to benefit from a downward movement in the market would be to sell stock short. The problem with shorting stock is you're exposed to theoretically unlimited risk if the stock price rises.

Puts may be used as an alternative to shorting stock, because they limit your risk to the cost of the options. If the stock goes up – the worst-case scenario – you don't have to deliver shares to the investor from whom you borrowed them, as with short stock. You simply allow your puts to expire or sell them to close your position (that is, if they're still worth something).

But be careful, especially with short-term out-of-the-money puts. If you buy too many option contracts, you are actually increasing your risk. Options may expire worthless and you can lose your entire investment.

Puts can also be used to help protect the value of stocks you already own. These are called "protective puts." See Play Seven.

OPTIONS GUY'S TIPS:

☞ Don't go overboard with the leverage you can get when buying puts. A general rule of thumb is this: If you're used to selling 100 shares of stock short per trade, buy one put contract (1 contract = 100 shares). If you're comfortable selling 200 shares short, buy two put contracts, and so on.

☞ You may wish to consider buying an in-the-money put, since it's likely to have a greater delta (that is, changes in the option's value will correspond more closely with any change in the stock price). Try looking for a delta of -.80 or greater if possible. In-the-money options are more expensive because they have intrinsic value, but you get what you pay for.

BREAK-EVEN AT EXPIRATION

Strike A minus the cost of the put.

THE SWEET SPOT

The stock goes right in the tank.

MAXIMUM POTENTIAL PROFIT

There's a substantial profit potential. If the stock goes to zero you make the entire strike price minus the cost of the put contract. Keep in mind, however, stocks usually don't go to zero. So be realistic, and don't plan on buying an Italian sports car after just one trade.

MAXIMUM POTENTIAL LOSS

Risk is limited to the premium paid for the put.

MARGIN REQUIREMENT

After the trade is paid for, no additional margin is required.

AS TIME GOES BY

For this play, time decay is the enemy. It will negatively affect the value of the option you bought.

IMPLIED VOLATILITY

After the play is established, increasing implied volatility is your friend. It will increase the value of the option you bought. It also reflects an increased possibility of a price swing (without regard for direction).

CHECK YOUR PLAY WITH TRADEKING TOOLS

• Use the Profit + Loss Calculator to establish break-even points, evaluate how your strategy might change as expiration approaches, and analyze the Greeks.

• Remember: If options are cheap, they're usually cheap for a reason. Use the Probability Calculator to help you form an opinion on your option's chances of expiring in-the-money.

• Use the Technical Analysis Tool to look for bearish indicators.

SHORT CALL

AKA Naked Call; Uncovered Call

THE SETUP

- Sell a call, Strike Price A

- Generally, the stock price will be below Strike A

WHO SHOULD RUN IT

All-Stars only

NOTE: Uncovered short calls (selling a call on a stock you don't own) is only suited for the most advanced option traders. It is not a play for the faint of heart.

WHEN TO RUN IT

  You're bearish to neutral.

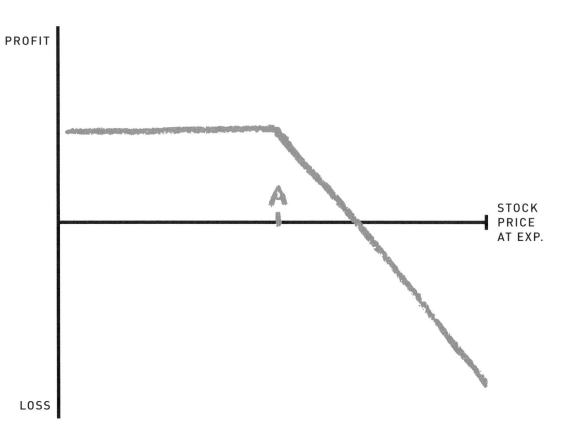

THE STRATEGY

Selling the call obligates you to sell stock at Strike Price A if the option is assigned.

When running this play, you want the call you sell to expire worthless. That's why most investors sell out-of-the-money options.

This play has a low profit potential if the stock remains below Strike A at expiration, but unlimited potential risk if the stock goes up. The reason some traders run this play is that there is a high probability for success when selling very out-of-the-money options. If the market moves against you, then you must have a stop-loss plan in place. Keep a watchful eye on this play as it unfolds.

👤 OPTIONS GUY'S TIPS:

☞ You may wish to consider ensuring that Strike A is one standard deviation or more out-of-the-money at initiation. That will increase your probability of success. However, the higher the strike price, the lower the premium received will be from this play.

☞ Some investors may wish to run this play using index options rather than options on individual stocks. That's because historically, indexes have not been as volatile as individual stocks. Fluctuations in an index's component stock prices tend to cancel one another out, lessening the volatility of the index as a whole.

ⓞ BREAK-EVEN AT EXPIRATION

Strike A plus the premium received for the call.

$ THE SWEET SPOT

There's a large sweet spot. As long as the stock price is at or below Strike A at expiration, you make your maximum profit. That's why this strategy is enticing to some traders.

⬆ MAXIMUM POTENTIAL PROFIT

Potential profit is limited to the premium received for selling the call.

⬇ MAXIMUM POTENTIAL LOSS

Risk is theoretically unlimited. If the stock keeps rising, you keep losing money. You may lose some hair as well. So hold onto your hat and stick to your stop-loss if the trade doesn't go your way.

% MARGIN REQUIREMENT

See Appendix A for margin requirement.

☯ AS TIME GOES BY

For this play, time decay is your friend. You want the price of the option you sold to approach zero. That means if you choose to close your position prior to expiration, it will be less expensive to buy it back.

⚡ IMPLIED VOLATILITY

After the play is established, increasing implied volatility is the enemy. It will increase the price of the option you sold. That means if you choose to close your position prior to expiration, it will be more expensive to buy it back.

✓ CHECK YOUR PLAY WITH TRADEKING TOOLS

• Use the Profit + Loss Calculator to establish break-even points, evaluate how your strategy might change as expiration approaches, and analyze the Greeks.

• Use the Probability Calculator to verify that the call you sell is at least one standard deviation out-of-the-money. (See Options Guy's Tips for more information.)

• Use the Technical Analysis tool to look for bearish indicators.

SHORT PUT

AKA Naked Put

THE SETUP

- Sell a put, Strike Price A

- Generally, the stock price will be above Strike A

WHO SHOULD RUN IT

All-Stars only

NOTE: Selling puts as pure speculation, with no intention of buying the stock, is suited only to the most advanced option traders. It is not a play for the faint of heart.

WHEN TO RUN IT

  You're bullish to neutral.

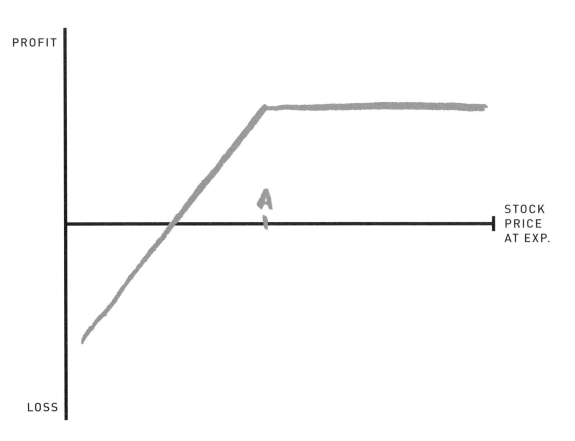

THE STRATEGY

Selling the put obligates you to buy stock at Strike Price A if the option is assigned.

When selling puts with no intention of buying the stock, you want the puts you sell to expire worthless. This play has a low profit potential if the stock remains above Strike A at expiration, but substantial potential risk if the stock goes down. The reason some traders run this play is that there is a high probability for success when selling very out-of-the-money puts. If the market moves against you, then you must have a stop-loss plan in place. Keep a watchful eye on this play as it unfolds.

👤 OPTIONS GUY'S TIPS:

☞ You may wish to consider ensuring that Strike A is one standard deviation or more out-of-the-money at initiation. That will increase your probability of success. However, the lower the strike price, the lower the premium received will be from this play.

☞ Some investors may wish to run this play using index options rather than options on individual stocks. That's because historically, indexes have not been as volatile as individual stocks. Fluctuations in an index's component stock prices tend to cancel one another out, lessening the volatility of the index as a whole.

⑪ BREAK-EVEN AT EXPIRATION

Strike A minus the premium received for the put.

$ THE SWEET SPOT

There's a large sweet spot. As long as the stock price is at or above Strike A at expiration, you make your maximum profit. That's why this strategy is enticing to some traders.

⬆ MAXIMUM POTENTIAL PROFIT

Potential profit is limited to the premium received for selling the put.

⬇ MAXIMUM POTENTIAL LOSS

Potential loss is substantial, but limited to the strike price minus the premium received if the stock goes to zero.

% MARGIN REQUIREMENT

See Appendix A for margin requirement.

⟳ AS TIME GOES BY

For this play, time decay is your friend. You want the price of the option you sold to approach zero. That means if you choose to close your position prior to expiration, it will be less expensive to buy it back.

⬌ IMPLIED VOLATILITY

After the play is established, increasing implied volatility is the enemy. It will increase the price of the option you sold. That means if you choose to close your position prior to expiration, it will be more expensive to buy it back.

✓ CHECK YOUR PLAY WITH TRADEKING TOOLS

• Use the Profit + Loss Calculator to establish break-even points, evaluate how your strategy might change as expiration approaches, and analyze the Greeks.

• Use the Probability Calculator to verify that the put you sell is at least one standard deviation out-of-the-money. (See Options Guy's Tips for more information.)

• Use the Technical Analysis tool to look for bullish indicators.

CASH-SECURED PUT

THE SETUP

• Sell a put, Strike Price A

• Keep enough cash on hand to buy the stock if the put is assigned

• Generally, the stock price will be above Strike A

WHO SHOULD RUN IT

Rookies or higher

NOTE: Cash-secured puts can be executed by investors at any level. See the "Rookie's Corner" for a more in-depth explanation of this play.

WHEN TO RUN IT

  You're slightly bearish short-term; bullish long-term.

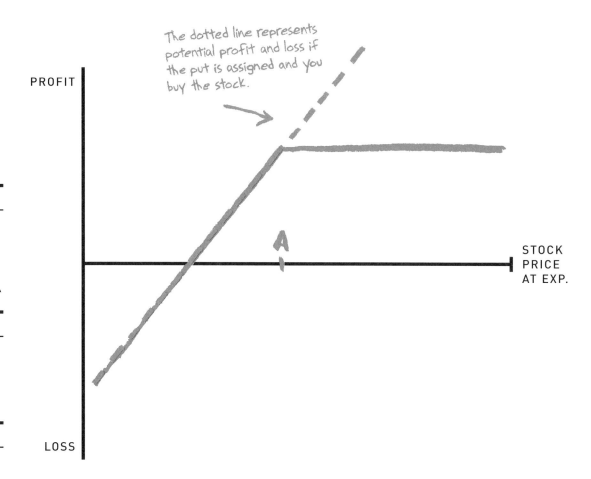

The dotted line represents potential profit and loss if the put is assigned and you buy the stock.

NOTE: This graph shows profit and loss of long stock and the short put.

THE STRATEGY

Selling the put obligates you to buy stock at Strike Price A if the option is assigned.

In this instance, you're selling the put with the intention of buying the stock after the put is assigned. When running this play, you may wish to consider selling the put slightly out-of-the-money. If you do so, you're hoping that the stock will make a bearish move, dip below the strike price, and stay there. That way the put will be assigned and you'll end up owning the stock. Naturally, you'll want the stock to rise in the long-term.

The premium received for the put you sell will lower the cost basis on the stock you want to buy. If the stock doesn't make a bearish move, you still keep the premium for selling the put. That's sort of nice, because it's one of the few instances when you can profit by being wrong.

OPTIONS GUY'S TIPS:

☞ Don't go overboard with the leverage you can get when selling puts. A general rule of thumb is this: If you're used to buying 100 shares of stock per trade, sell one put contract (1 contract = 100 shares). If you're comfortable buying 200 shares short, sell two put contracts, and so on.

BREAK-EVEN AT EXPIRATION

Strike A minus the premium received for the put.

THE SWEET SPOT

You want the stock price to be just below Strike A at expiration. Remember, the goal here is to wind up owning the stock.

MAXIMUM POTENTIAL PROFIT

Potential profit is limited to the premium received from selling the put. (If the puts are assigned, potential profit is changed to a "long stock" position.)

MAXIMUM POTENTIAL LOSS

Potential loss is substantial, but limited to the strike price if the stock goes to zero. (If the puts are assigned, potential loss is changed to a "long stock" position.)

MARGIN REQUIREMENT

See Appendix A for margin requirement.

AS TIME GOES BY

For this play, time decay is your friend. You want the price of the option you sold to approach zero. That means if you choose to close your position prior to expiration, it will be less expensive to buy it back.

IMPLIED VOLATILITY

After the play is established, increasing implied volatility is the enemy. It will increase the price of the option you sold. That means if you choose to close your position prior to expiration, it will be more expensive to buy it back.

CHECK YOUR PLAY WITH TRADEKING TOOLS

• Use the Profit + Loss Calculator to establish break-even points, evaluate how your strategy might change as expiration approaches, and analyze the Greeks.

• Look at stock fundamentals on TradeKing's research page. The idea is to hold the stock longer-term, so you need to be comfortable with that.

COVERED CALL

THE SETUP

- You own the stock
- Sell a call, Strike Price A
- Generally, the stock price will be below Strike A

WHO SHOULD RUN IT

Rookies or higher

NOTE: Covered calls can be executed by investors at any level. See the "Rookie's Corner" for a more in-depth explanation of this play.

WHEN TO RUN IT

  You're neutral to bullish, and you're willing to sell stock if it reaches a specific price.

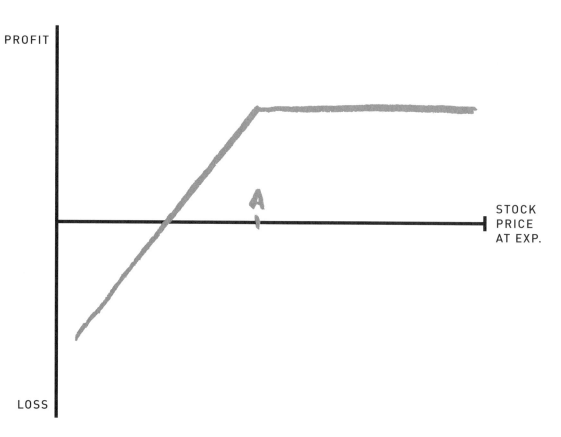

NOTE: This graph indicates profit and loss at expiration, respective to the stock value when you sold the call.

THE STRATEGY

Selling the call obligates you to sell stock you already own at Strike Price A if the option is assigned.

Some investors will run this play after they've already seen nice gains on the stock. Often, they will sell out-of-the-money calls, so if the stock price goes up, they're willing to part with the stock and take the profit.

Covered calls can also be used to achieve income on the stock above and beyond any dividends. The goal in that case is for the options to expire worthless.

If you buy the stock and sell the calls all at the same time, it's called a "Buy / Write." Some investors use a Buy / Write as a way to lower the cost basis of a stock they've just purchased.

OPTIONS GUY'S TIPS:

☞ As a general rule of thumb, you may wish to consider running this play approximately 30-45 days from expiration to take advantage of accelerating time decay as expiration approaches. Of course, this depends on the underlying stock and market conditions such as implied volatility.

☞ You may wish to consider selling the call with a premium that represents at least 2% of the current stock price (premium ÷ stock price). But ultimately, it's up to you what premium will make running this play worth your while.

☞ Beware of receiving too much time premium. If the premium seems abnormally high, there's usually a reason for it. Check for news in the marketplace that may affect the price of the stock. Remember, if something seems too good to be true, it usually is.

ⓝ BREAK-EVEN AT EXPIRATION

Current stock price minus the premium received for selling the call.

ⓢ THE SWEET SPOT

The sweet spot for this strategy depends on your objective. If you are selling covered calls to earn income on your stock, then you want the stock to remain as close to the strike price as possible without going above it.

If you want to sell the stock while making additional profit by selling the calls, then you want the stock to rise above the strike price and stay there at expiration. That way, the calls will be assigned.

However, you probably don't want the stock to shoot too high, or you might be a bit disappointed that you parted with it. But don't fret if that happens. You still made out all right on the stock. Do yourself a favor and stop getting quotes on it.

⬆ MAXIMUM POTENTIAL PROFIT

When the call is first sold, potential profit is limited to the strike price minus the current stock price plus the premium received for selling the call.

⬇ MAXIMUM POTENTIAL LOSS

You receive a premium for selling the option, but most downside risk comes from owning the stock, which may potentially lose its value. However, selling the option does create an "opportunity risk." That is, if the stock price skyrockets, the calls might be assigned and you'll miss out on those gains.

⅌ MARGIN REQUIREMENT

Because you own the stock, no additional margin is required.

⊗ AS TIME GOES BY

For this play, time decay is your friend. You want the price of the option you sold to approach zero. That means if you choose to close your position prior to expiration, it will be less expensive to buy it back.

⊕ IMPLIED VOLATILITY

After the play is established, increasing implied volatility is the enemy. It will increase the price of the option you sold. That means if you choose to close your position prior to expiration, it will be more expensive to buy it back.

✓ CHECK YOUR PLAY WITH TRADEKING TOOLS

• Use the Profit + Loss Calculator to establish break-even points, evaluate how your strategy might change as expiration approaches, and analyze the Greeks.

• View the Option Chains for your stock. Select the covered call option chain, and review the "Static Return" and "If Called Return" columns to make sure you're happy with potential outcomes. Static Return assumes the stock price is unchanged at expiration and the call expires worthless. If Called Return assumes the stock price rises above the strike price and the call is assigned.

PROTECTIVE PUT

THE SETUP

- You own the stock

- Buy a put, Strike Price A

- Generally, the stock price will be above Strike A

WHO SHOULD RUN IT

Rookies or higher

WHEN TO RUN IT

 You're bullish but nervous.

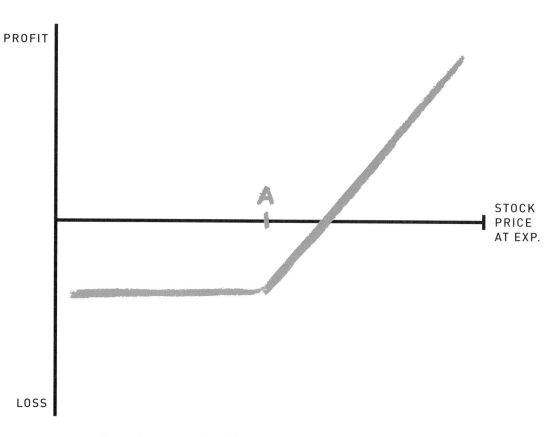

NOTE: This graph indicates profit and loss at expiration, respective to the stock value when you bought the put.

THE STRATEGY

Purchasing a protective put gives you the right to sell stock you already own at Strike Price A.

That can help protect the value of stocks in your portfolio in the event of a downturn. It'll also help you cut back on your antacid intake in times of market uncertainty.

Protective puts are often used as an alternative to stop orders. The problem with stop orders is they sometimes work when you don't want them to work, and when you really need them they don't work at all. For example, if a stock's price is fluctuating but not really tanking, a stop order might get you out prematurely. If that happens, you probably won't be too happy if the stock bounces back. Or, if a major news event happens overnight and the stock gaps down significantly on the open, you might not get out at your stop price. Instead, you'll get out at the next available market price, which could be much lower.

If you buy a protective put, you have complete control over when you exercise your option, and the price you're going to receive for your stock is predetermined. However, these benefits do come at a cost. It would be nice if the stock goes up at least enough to cover the premium paid for the put.

If you buy stock and a protective put at the same time, this is commonly referred to as a "married put." For added enjoyment, feel free to play a wedding march and throw rice while making this trade.

🧑 OPTIONS GUY'S TIPS:

☞ Many investors will buy a protective put when they've seen a nice run-up on the stock price, and they want to protect their unrealized profits against a downturn. It's sometimes easier to part with the money to pay for the put when you've already seen decent gains on the stock.

⓪ BREAK-EVEN AT EXPIRATION

From the point the protective put is established, the break-even point is the current stock price plus the premium paid for the put.

$ THE SWEET SPOT

You want the stock to go to infinity and the puts to expire worthless.

⬆ MAXIMUM POTENTIAL PROFIT

Potential profit is theoretically unlimited, because you'll still own the stock and you have not capped the upside.

⬇ MAXIMUM POTENTIAL LOSS

Risk is limited to the "deductible" (current stock price minus the strike price) plus the premium paid for the put.

% MARGIN REQUIREMENT

After the trade is paid for, no additional margin is required.

⏱ AS TIME GOES BY

For this play, time decay is the enemy. It will negatively affect the value of the option you bought.

⊕ IMPLIED VOLATILITY

After the play is established, increasing implied volatility is your friend. It will increase the value of the option you bought.

✔ CHECK YOUR PLAY WITH TRADEKING TOOLS

• Use the Profit + Loss Calculator to establish break-even points, evaluate how your strategy might change as expiration approaches, and analyze the Greeks.

COLLAR

THE SETUP

• You own the stock

• Buy a put, Strike Price A

• Sell a call, Strike Price B

• Generally, the stock price will be between Strikes A and B

NOTE: Both options have the same expiration month.

WHO SHOULD RUN IT

Rookies and up

WHEN TO RUN IT

 You're bullish but nervous.

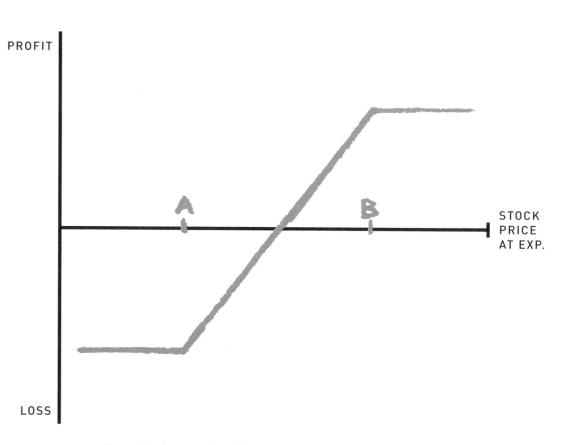

NOTE: This graph indicates profit and loss at expiration, respective to the stock value when you sold the call and bought the put.

THE STRATEGY

Buying the put gives you the right to sell the stock at Strike Price A. Because you've also sold the call, you'll be obligated to sell the stock at Strike Price B if the option is assigned.

You can think of a collar as simultaneously running a protective put (Play Seven) and a covered call (Play Six). Some investors think this is a sexy trade because the covered call helps to pay for the protective put. So you've limited the downside on the stock for less than it would cost to buy a put alone, but there's a trade-off.

The call you sell caps the upside. If the stock has exceeded Strike B by expiration, it will most likely be called away. So you must be willing to sell it at that price.

👤 OPTIONS GUY'S TIPS:

☞ Many investors will run a collar when they've seen a nice run-up on the stock price, and they want to protect their unrealized profits against a downturn.

☞ Some investors will try to sell the call with enough premium to pay for the put entirely. If established for net-zero cost, it is often referred to as a "zero-cost collar." It may even be established for a net credit, if the call with Strike Price B is worth more than the put with Strike Price A.

☞ Some investors will establish this play in a single trade. For every 100 shares they buy, they'll sell one out-of-the-money call contract and buy one out-of-the-money put contract. This limits your downside risk instantly, but of course, it also limits your upside.

🕐 BREAK-EVEN AT EXPIRATION

From the point the collar is established, there are two break-even points:

• If established for a net credit, the break-even is current stock price minus net credit received.

• If established for a net debit, the break-even is current stock price plus the net debit paid.

💲 THE SWEET SPOT

You want the stock price to be above Strike B at expiration and have the stock called away.

⬆ MAXIMUM POTENTIAL PROFIT

From the point the collar is established, potential profit is limited to Strike B minus current stock price minus the net debit paid, or plus net credit received.

⬇ MAXIMUM POTENTIAL LOSS

From the point the collar is established, risk is limited to the current stock price minus Strike A minus the net debit paid, or plus the net credit received.

% MARGIN REQUIREMENT

Because you own the stock, no additional margin is required after the trade is paid for (if established for a net debit).

🕐 AS TIME GOES BY

For this play, the net effect of time decay is somewhat neutral. It will erode the value of the option you bought (bad) but it will also erode the value of the option you sold (good).

⊕ IMPLIED VOLATILITY

After the play is established, the net effect of an increase in implied volatility is somewhat neutral. The option you sold will increase in value (bad), but it will also increase the value of the option you bought (good).

✅ CHECK YOUR PLAY WITH TRADEKING TOOLS

• Use the Profit and Loss Calculator to establish break-even points, evaluate how your strategy might change as expiration approaches, and analyze the Greeks.

LONG STRADDLE

THE SETUP

- Buy a call, Strike Price A
- Buy a put, Strike Price A
- Generally, the stock price will be at Strike A

NOTE: Both options have the same expiration month.

WHO SHOULD RUN IT

Seasoned Veterans or higher

NOTE: At first glance, this seems like a fairly simple play. However, it is not suited for all investors. To profit from a long straddle you'll require fairly advanced forecasting ability, for reasons we'll explain.

WHEN TO RUN IT

(?) You're anticipating a swing in stock price, but you're not sure which direction it will go.

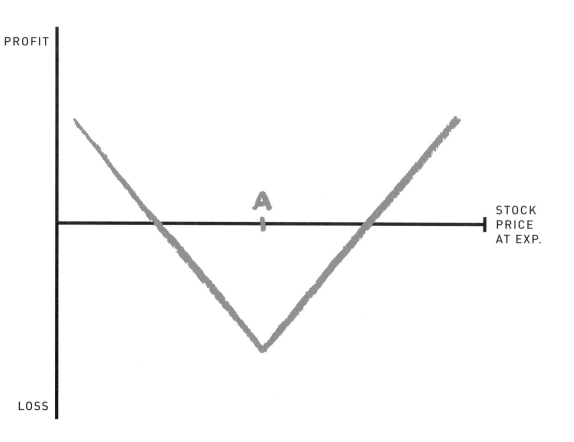

THE STRATEGY

A long straddle is the best of both worlds, since the call gives you the right to buy the stock at Strike Price A and the put gives you the right to sell the stock at Strike Price A. But those rights don't come cheap.

The goal is to profit if the stock moves in either direction. Typically, a straddle will be constructed with the call and put at-the-money (or at the nearest strike price if there's not one exactly at-the-money). Buying both a call and a put increases the cost of your position, especially for a volatile stock. So you'll need a fairly significant price swing just to break even.

Advanced traders might run this play to take advantage of a possible increase in implied volatility. If implied volatility is abnormally low for no apparent reason, the call and put may be undervalued. The idea is to buy them at a discount, then wait for implied volatility to rise and close the position at a profit.

OPTIONS GUY'S TIPS:

Many investors who use the long straddle will look for major news events that may cause the stock to make an abnormally large move. For example, they'll consider running this play prior to an earnings announcement that might send the stock in either direction.

If buying a short-term straddle (perhaps two weeks or less) prior to an earnings announcement, look at the stock's charts on TradeKing.com. There's a checkbox that allows you to see the dates when earnings were announced. Look for instances where the stock moved at least 1.5 times more than the cost of your straddle. If the stock didn't move at least that much on any of the last three earnings announcements, you probably shouldn't run this play. Lie down until the urge goes away.

BREAK-EVEN POINTS AT EXPIRATION

There are two break-even points:

- Strike A plus the net debit paid.
- Strike A minus the net debit paid.

THE SWEET SPOT

The stock shoots to the moon, or goes straight down the toilet.

MAXIMUM POTENTIAL PROFIT

Potential profit is theoretically unlimited if the stock goes up.

If the stock goes down, potential profit may be substantial but limited to the strike price minus the net debit paid.

MAXIMUM POTENTIAL LOSS

Potential losses are limited to the net debit paid.

MARGIN REQUIREMENT

After the trade is paid for, no additional margin is required.

AS TIME GOES BY

For this play, time decay is your mortal enemy. It will cause the value of both options to decrease, so it's working doubly against you.

IMPLIED VOLATILITY

After the play is established, increasing implied volatility is your best friend. It will increase the value of both options, and it also suggests an increased possibility of a price swing. Huzzah.

CHECK YOUR PLAY WITH TRADEKING TOOLS

- Use the Profit + Loss Calculator to establish break-even points, evaluate how your strategy might change as expiration approaches, and analyze the Greeks.

- Examine the stock's Volatility Charts. If you're doing this as a volatility play, you want to see implied volatility abnormally low compared to historic volatility.

SHORT STRADDLE

THE SETUP

- Sell a call, Strike Price A

- Sell a put, Strike Price A

- Generally, the stock price will be at Strike A

NOTE: Both options have the same expiration month.

WHO SHOULD RUN IT

All-Stars only

NOTE: This play is only suited for the most advanced traders and not for the faint of heart. Short straddles are mainly for market professionals who watch their account full-time. In other words, this is not a trade you manage from the golf course.

WHEN TO RUN IT

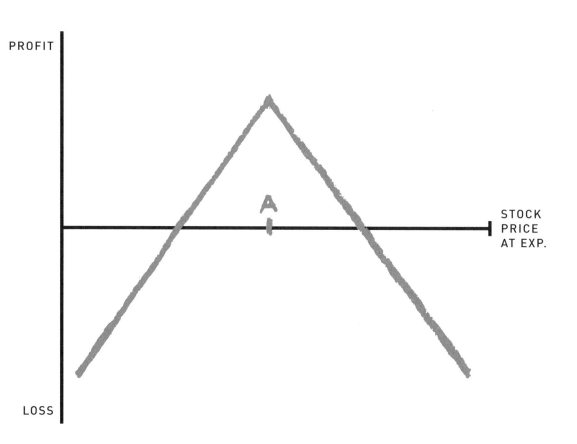

N You're expecting minimal movement on the stock. (In fact, you should be darn certain that the stock will stick close to Strike A.)

THE STRATEGY

A short straddle gives you the obligation to sell the stock at Strike Price A and the obligation to buy the stock at Strike Price A if the options are assigned.

By selling two options, you significantly increase the income you would have achieved from selling a put or a call alone. But that comes at a cost. You have unlimited risk on the upside and substantial downside risk.

Advanced traders might run this play to take advantage of a possible decrease in implied volatility. If implied volatility is abnormally high for no apparent reason, the call and put may be overvalued. After the sale, the idea is to wait for volatility to drop and close the position at a profit.

👤 OPTIONS GUY'S TIPS:

☞ Even if you're willing to accept high risk, you may wish to consider a short strangle (Play Twelve) since its sweet spot is wider than a short straddle's.

🔟 BREAK-EVEN AT EXPIRATION

There are two break-even points:

- Strike A minus the net credit received.

- Strike A plus the net credit received.

💲 THE SWEET SPOT

You want the stock exactly at Strike A at expiration, so the options expire worthless. However, that's extremely difficult to predict. Good luck with that.

⬆ MAXIMUM POTENTIAL PROFIT

Potential profit is limited to the net credit received for selling the call and the put.

⬇ MAXIMUM POTENTIAL LOSS

If the stock goes up, your losses could be theoretically unlimited.

If the stock goes down, your losses may be substantial, but limited to the strike price minus net credit received for selling the straddle.

％ MARGIN REQUIREMENT

See Appendix A for margin requirement.

🕐 AS TIME GOES BY

For this play, time decay is your best friend. It works doubly in your favor, eroding the price of both options you sold. That means if you choose to close your position prior to expiration, it will be less expensive to buy it back.

⚡ IMPLIED VOLATILITY

After the play is established, increasing implied volatility is your mortal enemy. It works doubly against you by increasing the price of both options you sold. That means if you wish to close your position prior to expiration, it will be more expensive to buy back the options.

An increase in implied volatility also suggests an increased possibility of a price swing, whereas you want the stock price to remain stable around Strike A.

✅ CHECK YOUR PLAY WITH TRADEKING TOOLS

- Use the Profit + Loss Calculator to establish break-even points, evaluate how your strategy might change as expiration approaches, and analyze the Greeks.

- Examine the stock's Volatility Charts. If you're doing this as a volatility play, you want to see implied volatility abnormally high compared with historic volatility.

LONG STRANGLE

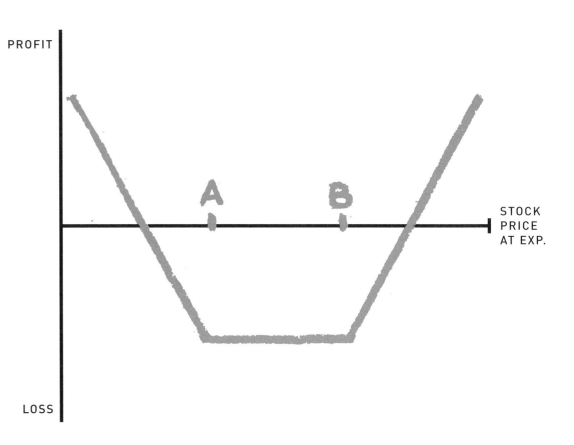

THE SETUP

- Buy a put, Strike Price A

- Buy a call, Strike Price B

- Generally, the stock price will be between Strikes A and B

NOTE: Both options have the same expiration month.

WHO SHOULD RUN IT

Seasoned Veterans or higher

NOTE: Like the long straddle (Play Nine), this seems like a fairly simple play. However, it is not suited for all investors. To profit from a long strangle you'll require fairly advanced forecasting ability, for reasons we'll explain.

WHEN TO RUN IT

You're anticipating a swing in stock price, but you're not sure which direction it will go.

THE STRATEGY

A long strangle gives you the right to sell the stock at Strike Price A and the right to buy the stock at Strike Price B.

The goal is to profit if the stock makes a move in either direction. However, buying both a call and a put increases the cost of your position, especially for a volatile stock. So you'll need a significant price swing just to break even.

The difference between a long strangle and a long straddle (Play Nine) is that you separate the strike prices for the two legs of the trade. That reduces the net cost of running this play, since the options you buy will be out-of-the-money. The tradeoff is, because we're dealing with an out-of-the-money call and an out-of-the-money put, the stock will need to move even more significantly before you make a profit.

👤 OPTIONS GUY'S TIPS:

☞ Many investors who use the long straddle will look for major news events that may cause the stock to make an abnormally large move. For example, they'll consider running this play prior to an earnings announcement that might send the stock in either direction.

☞ Because the stock will have to make such a significant move just to break even, you may wish to consider a long straddle instead even though it costs more to run.

🔟 BREAK-EVEN AT EXPIRATION

There are two break-even points:

- Strike A minus the net debit paid.
- Strike B plus the net debit paid.

💲 THE SWEET SPOT

The stock shoots to the moon, or goes straight down the toilet.

⬆ MAXIMUM POTENTIAL PROFIT

Potential profit is theoretically unlimited if the stock goes up.

If the stock goes down, potential profit may be substantial, but limited to Strike A minus the net debit paid.

⬇ MAXIMUM POTENTIAL LOSS

Potential losses are limited to the net debit paid.

% MARGIN REQUIREMENT

After the trade is paid for, no additional margin is required.

✺ AS TIME GOES BY

For this play, time decay is your mortal enemy. It will cause the value of both options to decrease, so it's working doubly against you.

⟐ IMPLIED VOLATILITY

After the play is established, increasing implied volatility is your best friend. It will increase the value of your options, and it also suggests an increased possibility of a price swing. Sweet.

✔ CHECK YOUR PLAY WITH TRADEKING TOOLS

- Use the Profit + Loss Calculator to establish break-even points, evaluate how your strategy might change as expiration approaches, and analyze the Greeks.

SHORT STRANGLE

THE SETUP

- Sell a put, Strike Price A

- Sell a call, Strike Price B

- Generally, the stock price will be between Strikes A and B

NOTE: Both options have the same expiration month.

WHO SHOULD RUN IT

All-Stars only

NOTE: This play is only for the most advanced traders who like to live dangerously (and watch their accounts constantly).

WHEN TO RUN IT

 You are anticipating minimal movement on the stock.

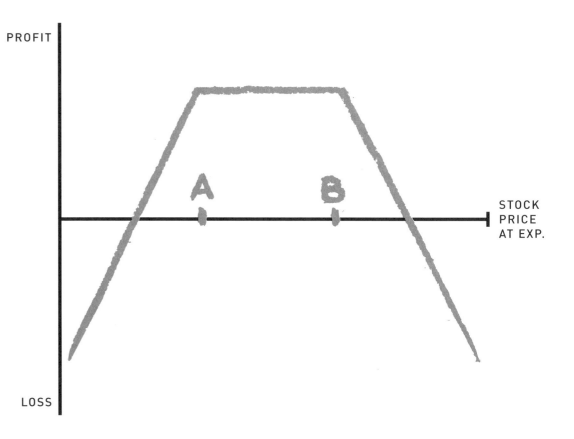

THE STRATEGY

A short strangle gives you the obligation to buy the stock at Strike Price A and the obligation to sell the stock at Strike Price B if the options are assigned. You are predicting the stock price will remain somewhere between Strike A and Strike B, and the options you sell will expire worthless.

By selling two options, you significantly increase the income you would have achieved from selling a put or a call alone. But that comes at a cost. You have unlimited risk on the upside and substantial downside risk. To avoid being exposed to such risk, you may wish to consider using a long iron condor instead (Play Twenty-Six).

Like the short straddle (Play Ten), advanced traders might run this play to take advantage of a possible decrease in implied volatility. If implied volatility is abnormally high for no apparent reason, the call and put may be overvalued. After the sale, the idea is to wait for volatility to drop and close the position at a profit.

OPTIONS GUY'S TIPS:

☞ You may wish to consider ensuring that Strike A and Strike B are one standard deviation or more away from the stock price at initiation. That will increase your probability of success. However, the further out-of-the-money the strike prices are, the lower the net credit received will be from this play.

⑩ BREAK-EVEN AT EXPIRATION

There are two break-even points:

- Strike A minus the net credit received.

- Strike B plus the net credit received.

$ THE SWEET SPOT

You want the stock at or between Strikes A and B at expiration, so the options expire worthless.

⬆ MAXIMUM POTENTIAL PROFIT

Potential profit is limited to the net credit received

⬇ MAXIMUM POTENTIAL LOSS

If the stock goes up, your losses could be theoretically unlimited.

If the stock goes down, your losses may be substantial, but limited to Strike A minus the net credit received.

% MARGIN REQUIREMENT

See Appendix A for margin requirement.

☽ AS TIME GOES BY

For this play, time decay is your best friend. It works doubly in your favor, eroding the price of both options you sold. That means if you choose to close your position prior to expiration, it will be less expensive to buy it back.

⬆ IMPLIED VOLATILITY

After the play is established, increasing implied volatility is your mortal enemy. It works doubly against you by increasing the price of both options you sold. That means if you wish to close your position prior to expiration, it will be more expensive to buy back the options.

An increase in implied volatility also suggests an increased possibility of a price swing, whereas you want the stock price to remain stable between Strike A and Strike B.

✓ CHECK YOUR PLAY WITH TRADEKING TOOLS

- Use the Profit + Loss Calculator to establish break-even points, evaluate how your strategy might change as expiration approaches, and analyze the Greeks.

- Use the Probability Calculator to verify that both the call and put you sell are at least one standard deviation (if not more) out-of-the-money. (See Options Guy's Tips for more.)

- Examine the stock's Volatility Charts. If you're doing this as a volatility play, you want to see implied volatility abnormally high compared with historic volatility.

LONG CALL SPREAD

AKA Bull Call Spread; Vertical Spread

THE SETUP

- Buy a call, Strike Price A

- Sell a call, Strike Price B

- Generally, the stock will be at or above Strike A and below Strike B

NOTE: Both options have the same expiration month.

WHO SHOULD RUN IT

Veterans or higher

WHEN TO RUN IT

 You're bullish, but you have an upside target.

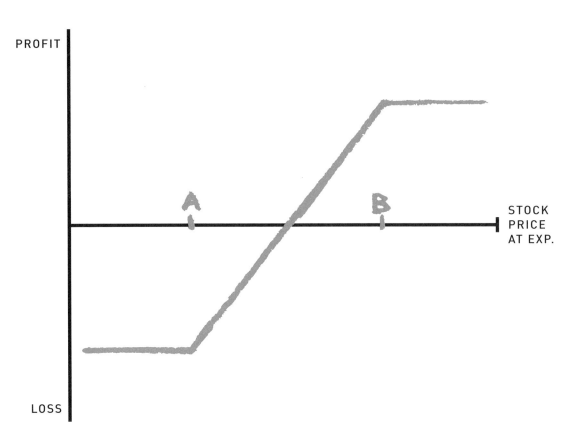

THE STRATEGY

A long call spread gives you the right to buy stock at Strike Price A and obligates you to sell the stock at Strike Price B if assigned.

This play is an alternative to buying a long call (Play One). Selling a cheaper call with higher-Strike B helps to offset the cost of the call you buy at Strike A. That ultimately limits your risk. The bad news is, to get the reduction in risk, you're going to have to sacrifice some potential profit.

👤 OPTIONS GUY'S TIPS:

☞ Because you're both buying and selling a call, the potential effect of a decrease in implied volatility will be somewhat neutralized.

☞ The maximum value of a long call spread is usually achieved when it's close to expiration. If you choose to close your position prior to expiration, you'll want as little time value as possible remaining on the call you sold. You may wish to consider buying a shorter-term long call spread, e.g. 30-45 days from expiration.

⑩ BREAK-EVEN AT EXPIRATION

Strike A plus net debit paid.

💲 THE SWEET SPOT

You want the stock to be at or above Strike B at expiration, but not so far that you're disappointed you didn't simply buy a call on the underlying stock. But look on the bright side if that does happen – you played it smart and made a profit, and that's always a good thing.

⬆ MAXIMUM POTENTIAL PROFIT

Potential profit is limited to the difference between Strike A and Strike B minus the net debit paid.

⬇ MAXIMUM POTENTIAL LOSS

Risk is limited to the net debit paid.

% MARGIN REQUIREMENT

After the trade is paid for, no additional margin is required.

✺ AS TIME GOES BY

For this play, the net effect of time decay is somewhat neutral. It's eroding the value of the option you purchased (bad) and the option you sold (good).

✦ IMPLIED VOLATILITY

After the play is established, increasing implied volatility is somewhat neutral. It will increase the value of the option you bought (good) and the option you sold (bad). So if you choose to close your position prior to expiration, implied volatility is not a huge concern on this play.

✓ CHECK YOUR PLAY WITH TRADEKING TOOLS

• Use the Profit + Loss Calculator to establish break-even points, evaluate how your strategy might change as expiration approaches, and analyze the Greeks.

• Use the Technical Analysis Tool to look for bullish indicators.

SHORT CALL SPREAD

AKA Bear Call Spread; Vertical Spread

THE SETUP

- Sell a call, Strike Price A
- Buy a call, Strike Price B
- Generally, the stock will be below Strike A

NOTE: Both options have the same expiration month.

WHO SHOULD RUN IT

Seasoned Veterans or higher

WHEN TO RUN IT

 You're bearish. You may also be expecting neutral activity if Strike A is out-of-the-money.

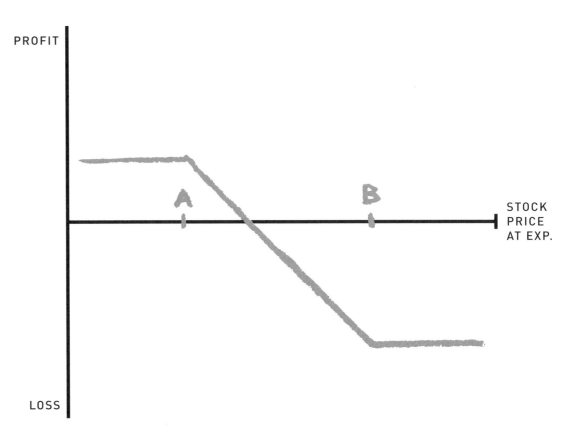

THE STRATEGY

A short call spread obligates you to sell the stock at Strike Price A if the option is assigned but gives you the right to buy stock at Strike Price B.

A short call spread is an alternative to the short call (Play Three). In addition to selling a call with Strike A, you're buying the cheaper call with Strike B to limit your risk if the stock goes up. But there's a tradeoff – buying the call also reduces the net credit received when running the play.

OPTIONS GUY'S TIPS:

☞ One advantage of this play is that you want both options to expire worthless. If that happens, you won't have to pay any commissions to get out of your position.

☞ You may wish to consider ensuring that Strike A is one standard deviation or more out-of-the-money at initiation. That will increase your probability of success. However, the further out-of-the-money the strike price is, the lower the net credit received will be from this play.

☞ As a general rule of thumb, you may wish to consider running this play approximately 30-45 days from expiration to take advantage of accelerating time decay as expiration approaches. Of course, this depends on the underlying stock and market conditions such as implied volatility.

BREAK-EVEN AT EXPIRATION

Strike A plus the net credit received when opening the position.

THE SWEET SPOT

You want the stock price to be at or below Strike A at expiration, so both options expire worthless.

MAXIMUM POTENTIAL PROFIT

Potential profit is limited to the net credit received when opening the position.

MAXIMUM POTENTIAL LOSS

Risk is limited to the difference between Strike A and Strike B, minus the net credit received.

MARGIN REQUIREMENT

See Appendix A for margin requirement.

AS TIME GOES BY

For this play, the net effect of time decay is somewhat positive. It will erode the value of the option you sold (good) but it will also erode the value of the option you bought (bad).

IMPLIED VOLATILITY

After the play is established, increasing implied volatility is somewhat negative. It will increase the value of both the option you sold (bad) and the option you bought (good).

CHECK YOUR PLAY WITH TRADEKING TOOLS

• Use the Profit + Loss Calculator to establish break-even points and evaluate how your strategy might change as expiration approaches, depending on the Greeks.

• Use the Technical Analysis Tool to look for bearish indicators.

• Use the Probability Calculator to verify that Strike A is approximately one standard deviation (or more) out-of-the-money. (See Options Guy's Tips for more information.)

LONG PUT SPREAD

AKA Bear Put Spread; Vertical Spread

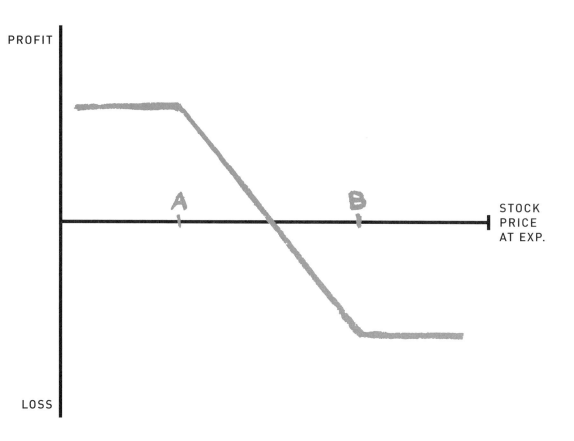

PROFIT

LOSS

A

B

STOCK PRICE AT EXP.

THE SETUP

• Sell a put, Strike Price A

• Buy a put, Strike Price B

• Generally, the stock will be at or below Strike B and above Strike A

NOTE: Both options have the same expiration month.

WHO SHOULD RUN IT

Veterans or higher

WHEN TO RUN IT

 You're bearish, with a downside target.

THE STRATEGY

A long put spread gives you the right to sell stock at Strike Price B and obligates you to buy stock at Strike Price A if assigned.

This play is an alternative to buying a long put (Play Two). Selling a cheaper put with Strike A helps to offset the cost of the put you buy with Strike B. That ultimately limits your risk. The bad news is, to get the reduction in risk, you're going to have to sacrifice some potential profit.

👤 OPTIONS GUY'S TIPS:

☞ When implied volatility is unusually high (e.g., around earnings) consider a long put spread as an alternative to merely buying a put alone. Because you're both buying and selling a put, the potential effect of a decrease in implied volatility will be somewhat neutralized.

☞ The maximum value of a long put spread is usually achieved when it's close to expiration. If you choose to close your position prior to expiration, you'll want as little time value as possible remaining on the put you sold. You may wish to consider buying a shorter-term long put spread, e.g. 30-45 days from expiration.

⑩ BREAK-EVEN AT EXPIRATION

Strike B minus the net debit paid.

Ⓢ THE SWEET SPOT

You want the stock to be at or below Strike A at expiration.

⬆ MAXIMUM POTENTIAL PROFIT

Potential profit is limited to the difference between Strike A and Strike B, minus the net debit paid.

⬇ MAXIMUM POTENTIAL LOSS

Risk is limited to the net debit paid.

﹪ MARGIN REQUIREMENT

After the trade is paid for, no additional margin is required.

✳ AS TIME GOES BY

For this play, the net effect of time decay is somewhat neutral. It's eroding the value of the option you bought (bad) and the option you sold (good).

✴ IMPLIED VOLATILITY

After the play is established, increasing implied volatility is somewhat neutral. It will increase the value of both the option you bought (good) and the option you sold (bad).

✅ CHECK YOUR PLAY WITH TRADEKING TOOLS

• Use the Profit + Loss Calculator to establish break-even points, evaluate how your strategy might change as expiration approaches, and analyze the Greeks.

• Use the Technical Analysis Tool to look for bearish indicators.

SHORT
PUT
SPREAD

AKA Bull Put Spread; Vertical Spread

THE SETUP

- Buy a put, Strike Price A
- Sell a put, Strike Price B
- Generally, the stock will be above Strike B

NOTE: Both options have the same expiration month.

WHO SHOULD RUN IT

Seasoned Veterans or higher

WHEN TO RUN IT

 You're bullish. You may also be anticipating neutral activity if Strike B is out-of-the-money.

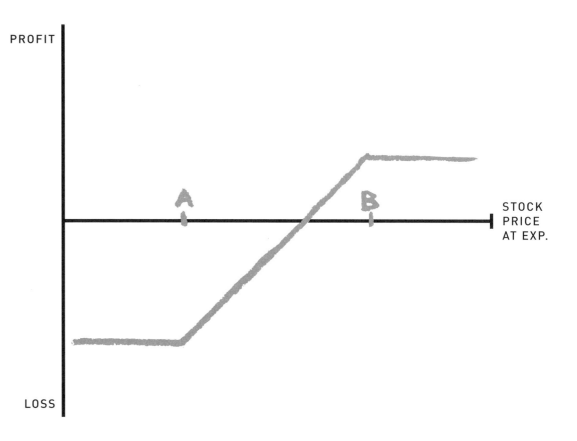

THE STRATEGY

A short put spread obligates you to buy the stock at Strike Price B if the option is assigned but gives you the right to sell stock at Strike Price A.

A short put spread is an alternative to the short put (Play Four). In addition to selling a put with Strike B, you're buying the cheaper put with Strike A to limit your risk if the stock goes down. But there's a tradeoff – buying the put also reduces the net credit received when running the play.

OPTIONS GUY'S TIPS:

☞ One advantage of this play is that you want both options to expire worthless. If that happens, you won't have to pay any commissions to get out of your position.

☞ You may wish to consider ensuring that Strike B is one standard deviation or more out-of-the-money at initiation. That will increase your probability of success. However, the further out-of-the-money the strike price is, the lower the net credit received will be from this spread.

☞ As a general rule of thumb, you may wish to consider running this play approximately 30-45 days from expiration to take advantage of accelerating time decay as expiration approaches. Of course, this depends on the underlying stock and market conditions such as implied volatility.

BREAK-EVEN AT EXPIRATION

Strike B minus the net credit received when selling the spread.

THE SWEET SPOT

You want the stock to be at or above Strike B at expiration, so both options will expire worthless.

MAXIMUM POTENTIAL PROFIT

Potential profit is limited to the net credit you receive when you set up the play.

MAXIMUM POTENTIAL LOSS

Risk is limited to the difference between Strike A and Strike B, minus the net credit received.

MARGIN REQUIREMENT

See Appendix A for margin requirement.

AS TIME GOES BY

For this play, the net effect of time decay is somewhat positive. It will erode the value of the option you sold (good) but it will also erode the value of the option you bought (bad).

IMPLIED VOLATILITY

After the play is established, increasing implied volatility is somewhat negative. It will increase the value of both the option you sold (bad) and the option you bought (good).

CHECK YOUR PLAY WITH TRADEKING TOOLS

• Use the Profit + Loss Calculator to establish break-even points and evaluate how your strategy might change as expiration approaches, depending on the Greeks.

• Use the Technical Analysis Tool to look for bullish indicators.

• Use the Probability Calculator to verify that Strike B is approximately one standard deviation (or more) out-of-the-money. (See Options Guy's Tips for more information.)

RATIO VERTICAL SPREAD W/ CALLS

AKA Call Front Spread

THE SETUP

- Buy a call, Strike Price A
- Sell two calls, Strike Price B
- Generally, the stock will be below or at Strike A

NOTE: All options have the same expiration month.

WHO SHOULD RUN IT

All-Stars only

NOTE: Due to the unlimited risk if the stock moves significantly higher, this play is suited only to the most advanced option traders.

WHEN TO RUN IT

You're slightly bullish. You want the stock to rise to Strike B and then stop.

NOTE: This graph assumes the play was established for a net credit.

THE STRATEGY

Buying the call gives you the right to buy stock at Strike Price A. Selling the two calls gives you the obligation to sell stock at Strike Price B if the options are assigned.

This play enables you to purchase a call that is at-the-money or slightly out-of-the-money without paying full price. The goal is to obtain the call with Strike A for a credit or a very small debit by selling the two calls with Strike B.

Ideally, you want a slight rise in stock price to Strike B. But watch out. Although one of the calls you sold is "covered" by the call you buy with Strike A, the second call you sold is "uncovered," exposing you to theoretically unlimited risk.

If the stock goes too high, you'll be in for a world of hurt. So beware of any abnormal moves in stock price and have a stop-loss plan in place.

OPTIONS GUY'S TIPS:

☞ Some investors may wish to run this play using index options rather than options on individual stocks. That's because historically, indexes have not been as volatile as individual stocks. Fluctuations in an index's component stock prices tend to cancel one another out, lessening the volatility of the index as a whole.

☞ The maximum value of a ratio vertical spread is usually achieved when it's close to expiration. You may wish to consider running this play shorter-term, e.g. 30-45 days from expiration.

☞ If you're not approved to sell uncovered calls, consider buying the stock at the same time you set up this play. That way, the second call won't be uncovered.

BREAK-EVEN AT EXPIRATION

If established for a net debit, there are two break-even points:

• Strike A plus net debit paid to establish the position.

• Strike B plus the maximum profit potential.

If established for a net credit, there is only one break-even point:

• Strike B plus the maximum profit potential.

THE SWEET SPOT

You want the stock price exactly at Strike B at expiration.

MAXIMUM POTENTIAL PROFIT

If established for a net debit, potential profit is limited to the difference between Strike A and Strike B, minus the net debit paid.

If established for a net credit, potential profit is limited to the difference between Strike A and Strike B, plus the net credit.

MAXIMUM POTENTIAL LOSS

If established for a net debit:

• Risk is limited to the debit paid for the spread if the stock price goes down.

• Risk is unlimited if the stock price goes way, way up.

If established for a net credit:

• Risk is unlimited if the stock price goes way, way up.

MARGIN REQUIREMENT

See Appendix A for margin requirement.

AS TIME GOES BY

For this play, time decay is your friend. It's eroding the value of the option you purchased (bad). However, that will be outweighed by the decrease in value of the two options you sold (good).

IMPLIED VOLATILITY

After the play is established, increasing implied volatility is somewhat negative. The value of the option you purchase will increase (good). However, that will be outweighed by the increase in value of the two options you sold (bad).

CHECK YOUR PLAY WITH TRADEKING TOOLS

• Use the Profit + Loss Calculator to establish break-even points, evaluate how your strategy might change as expiration approaches, and analyze the Greeks.

RATIO VERTICAL SPREAD W/ PUTS

AKA Put Front Spread

THE SETUP

- Sell two puts, Strike Price A

- Buy a put, Strike Price B

- Generally, the stock will be at or above Strike B.

NOTE: All options have the same expiration month.

WHO SHOULD RUN IT

All-Stars only

NOTE: Due to the significant risk if the stock moves sharply downward, this play is suited only to the most advanced option traders.

WHEN TO RUN IT

You're slightly bearish. You want the stock to go down to Strike A and then stop.

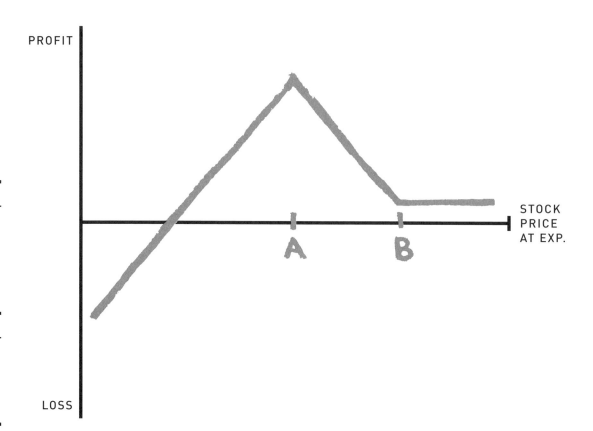

NOTE: This graph assumes the play was established for a net credit.

THE STRATEGY

Buying the put gives you the right to sell stock at Strike Price B. Selling the two puts gives you the obligation to buy stock at Strike Price A if the options are assigned.

This play enables you to purchase a put that is at-the-money or slightly out-of-the-money without paying full price. The goal is to obtain the put with Strike B for a credit or a very small debit by selling the two puts with Strike A.

Ideally, you want a slight dip in stock price to Strike A. But watch out. Although one of the puts you sold is "covered" by the put you buy with Strike B, the second put you sold is "uncovered," exposing you to significant downside risk.

If the stock goes too low, you'll be in for a world of hurt. So beware of any abnormal moves in stock price and have a stop-loss plan in place.

👤 OPTIONS GUY'S TIPS:

☞ Some investors may wish to run this play using index options rather than options on individual stocks. That's because historically, indexes have not been as volatile as individual stocks. Fluctuations in an index's component stock prices tend to cancel one another out, lessening the volatility of the index as a whole.

☞ The maximum value of a ratio vertical spread is usually achieved when it's close to expiration. You may wish to consider running this play shorter-term, e.g. 30-45 days from expiration.

🔟 BREAK-EVEN AT EXPIRATION

If established for a net debit, there are two break-even points:

- Strike B minus the net debit paid to establish the position.

- Strike A minus the maximum profit potential.

If established for a net credit, there is only one break-even point:

- Strike A minus the maximum profit potential.

💲 THE SWEET SPOT

You want the stock price exactly at Strike A at expiration.

⬆ MAXIMUM POTENTIAL PROFIT

If established for a net debit, potential profit is limited to the difference between Strike A and Strike B, minus the net debit paid.

If established for a net credit, potential profit is limited to the difference between Strike A and Strike B plus the net credit.

⬇ MAXIMUM POTENTIAL LOSS

If established for a net debit:

- Risk is limited to the net debit paid if the stock price goes up.

- Risk is substantial but limited to Strike A plus the net debit paid if the stock goes to zero.

If established for a net credit:

- Risk is substantial but limited to Strike A minus the net credit if the stock goes to zero.

% MARGIN REQUIREMENT

See Appendix A for margin requirement.

🌑 AS TIME GOES BY

For this play, time decay is your friend. It's eroding the value of the option you purchased (bad). However, that will be outweighed by the decrease in value of the two options you sold (good).

💠 IMPLIED VOLATILITY

After the play is established, increasing implied volatility is somewhat negative. The value of the option you purchase will increase (good). However, that will be outweighed by the increase in value of the two options you sold (bad).

✔ CHECK YOUR PLAY WITH TRADEKING TOOLS

- Use the Profit + Loss Calculator to establish break-even points, evaluate how your strategy might change as expiration approaches, and analyze the Greeks.

LONG BUTTERFLY SPREAD W/ CALLS

THE SETUP

- Buy a call, Strike Price A

- Sell two calls, Strike Price B

- Buy a call, Strike Price C

- Generally, the stock will be at Strike B

NOTE: Strike prices are equidistant, and all options have the same expiration month.

WHO SHOULD RUN IT

Seasoned Veterans and higher

NOTE: Due to the narrow sweet spot and the fact you're trading three different options in one play, butterfly spreads may be better suited for more advanced option traders.

WHEN TO RUN IT

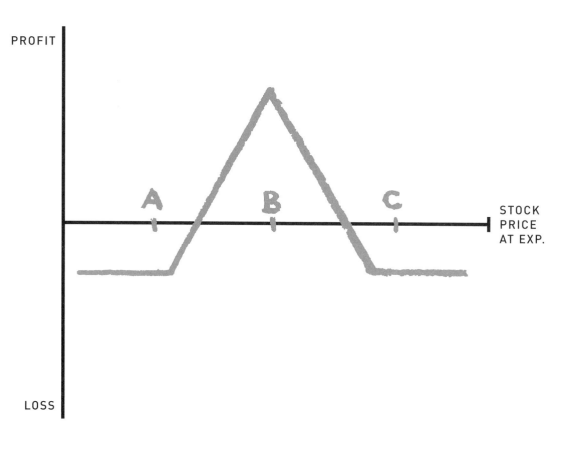

Typically, investors will use butterfly spreads when anticipating minimal movement on the stock within a specific time frame.

THE STRATEGY

A long butterfly spread with calls is a combination of a long call spread (Play Thirteen) and a short call spread (Play Fourteen), with the spreads converging at Strike Price B.

Ideally, you want the calls with Strikes B and C to expire worthless while capturing the intrinsic value of the in-the-money call with Strike A.

Because you're selling the two options with Strike B, butterflies are a relatively low-cost strategy. So the risk vs. reward can be tempting. However, the odds of hitting the sweet spot are fairly low.

Constructing your butterfly spread with Strike B slightly in-the-money or slightly out-of-the-money may make it a bit less expensive to run. This will put a directional bias on the trade. If Strike B is higher than the stock price, this would be considered a bullish trade. If Strike B is below the stock price, it would be a bearish trade. (But for simplicity's sake, if bearish, puts would usually be used to construct the spread).

👤 OPTIONS GUY'S TIPS:

👉 Some investors may wish to run this play using index options rather than options on individual stocks. That's because historically, indexes have not been as volatile as individual stocks. Fluctuations in an index's component stock prices tend to cancel one another out, lessening the volatility of the index as a whole.

🔟 BREAK-EVEN AT EXPIRATION

There are two break-even points for this play:

- Strike A plus the net debit paid.
- Strike C minus the net debit paid.

💲 THE SWEET SPOT

You want the stock price to be exactly at Strike B at expiration.

⬆ MAXIMUM POTENTIAL PROFIT

Potential profit is limited to Strike B minus Strike A minus the net debit paid.

⬇ MAXIMUM POTENTIAL LOSS

Risk is limited to the net debit paid.

% MARGIN REQUIREMENT

After the trade is paid for, no additional margin is required.

🕐 AS TIME GOES BY

For this play, time decay is your friend. Ideally, you want all options except the call with Strike A to expire worthless.

⊕ IMPLIED VOLATILITY

After the play is established, increasing implied volatility is the enemy. Your main concern is the at-the-money options you've sold. An increase in implied volatility will increase the price of these options, so if you choose to close your position prior to expiration, it will be more expensive to buy them back.

In addition, you want the stock price to remain stable, but an increase in implied volatility suggests an increased possibility of a price swing.

✔ CHECK YOUR PLAY WITH TRADEKING TOOLS

- Use the Profit + Loss Calculator to establish break-even points, evaluate how your strategy might change as expiration approaches, and analyze the Greeks.

LONG BUTTERFLY SPREAD W/ PUTS

THE SETUP

- Buy a put, Strike Price A
- Sell two puts, Strike Price B
- Buy a put, Strike Price C
- Generally, the stock will be at Strike B

NOTE: Strike prices are equidistant, and all options have the same expiration month.

WHO SHOULD RUN IT

Seasoned Veterans and higher

NOTE: Due to the narrow sweet spot and the fact you're trading three different options in one play, butterfly spreads may be better suited for more advanced option traders.

WHEN TO RUN IT

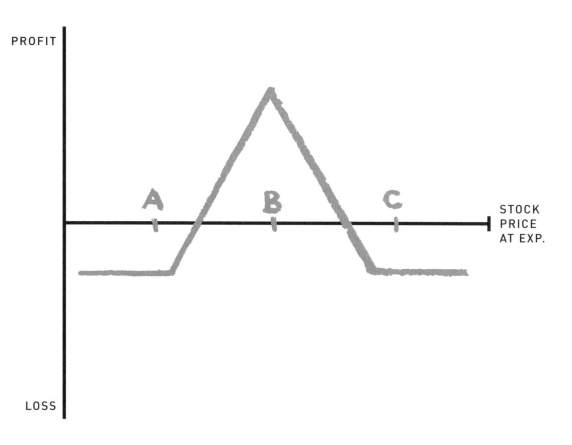

Typically, investors will use butterfly spreads when anticipating minimal movement on the stock within a specific time frame.

THE STRATEGY

A long butterfly spread with puts is a combination of a short put spread (Play Sixteen) and a long put spread (Play Fifteen), with the spreads converging at Strike B.

Ideally, you want the puts with Strikes A and B to expire worthless, while capturing the intrinsic value of the in-the-money put with Strike C.

Because you're selling two options with Strike B, butterflies are a relatively low-cost strategy. So the risk vs. reward can be tempting. However, the odds of hitting the sweet spot are fairly low.

Constructing your butterfly spread with Strike B slightly in-the-money or slightly out-of-the-money may make it a bit less expensive to run. This will put a directional bias on the trade. If Strike B is higher than the stock price, this would be considered a bullish trade. If Strike B is below the stock price, it would be a bearish trade. (But for simplicity's sake, if bullish, calls would usually be used to construct the spread).

👤 OPTIONS GUY'S TIPS:

☞ Some investors may wish to run this play using index options rather than options on individual stocks. That's because historically, indexes have not been as volatile as individual stocks. Fluctuations in an index's component stock prices tend to cancel one another out, lessening the volatility of the index as a whole.

⓾ BREAK-EVEN AT EXPIRATION

There are two break-even points for this play:

• Strike A plus the net debit paid.

• Strike C minus the net debit paid.

💲 THE SWEET SPOT

You want the stock price to be exactly at Strike B at expiration.

⬆ MAXIMUM POTENTIAL PROFIT

Potential profit is limited to Strike C minus Strike B minus the net debit paid.

⬇ MAXIMUM POTENTIAL LOSS

Risk is limited to the net debit paid.

% MARGIN REQUIREMENT

After the trade is paid for, no additional margin is required.

✷ AS TIME GOES BY

For this play, time decay is your friend. Ideally, you want all options except the put with Strike C to expire worthless.

⬦ IMPLIED VOLATILITY

After the play is established, increasing implied volatility is the enemy. Your main concern is the at-the-money options you've sold. An increase in implied volatility will increase the price of these options, so if you choose to close your position prior to expiration, it will be more expensive to buy them back.

In addition, you want the stock price to remain stable, but an increase in implied volatility suggests an increased possibility of a price swing.

✔ CHECK YOUR PLAY WITH TRADEKING TOOLS

• Use the Profit + Loss Calculator to establish break-even points, evaluate how your strategy might change as expiration approaches, and analyze the Greeks.

LONG IRON BUTTERFLY SPREAD

THE SETUP

- Buy a put, Strike Price A

- Sell a put, Strike Price B

- Sell a call, Strike Price B

- Buy a call, Strike Price C

- Generally, the stock will be at Strike B

NOTE: Strike prices are equidistant, and all options have the same expiration month.

WHO SHOULD RUN IT

Seasoned Veterans and higher

NOTE: Due to the narrow sweet spot and the fact you're trading four different options in one play, long iron butterfly spreads may be better suited for more advanced option traders.

WHEN TO RUN IT

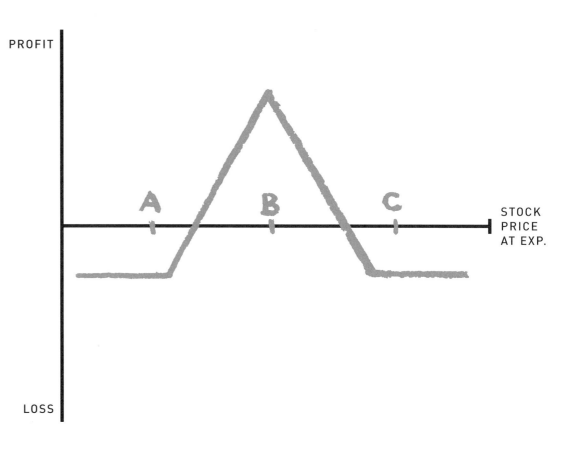

Typically, investors will use butterfly spreads when anticipating minimal movement on the stock within a specific time frame.

THE STRATEGY

You can think of this play as simultaneously running a short put spread (Play Sixteen) and a short call spread (Play Fourteen) with the spreads converging at Strike B. Because it's a combination of short spreads, Iron Butterflies can be established for a net credit.

Ideally, you want all of the options in this spread to expire worthless, with the stock at Strike B. However, the odds of this happening are fairly low, so you'll probably have to pay something to close your position.

It is possible to put a directional bias on this trade. If Strike B is higher than the stock price, this would be considered a bullish trade. If Strike B is below the stock price, it would be a bearish trade.

👤 OPTIONS GUY'S TIPS:

☞ Since a long iron butterfly is a "four-legged" spread, the commissions typically cost more than a long butterfly. That causes some investors to opt for the long butterfly instead. (However, since TradeKing's commissions are so low, this will hurt you less than it would with some other brokers.)

☞ Some investors may wish to run this play using index options rather than options on individual stocks. That's because historically, indexes have not been as volatile as individual stocks. Fluctuations in an index's component stock prices tend to cancel one another out, lessening the volatility of the index as a whole.

🔟 BREAK-EVEN AT EXPIRATION

There are two break-even points for this play:

• Strike B plus net credit received.

• Strike B minus net credit received.

💲 THE SWEET SPOT

You want the stock price to be exactly at Strike B at expiration so all four options expire worthless.

⬆ MAXIMUM POTENTIAL PROFIT

Potential profit is limited to the net credit received.

⬇ MAXIMUM POTENTIAL LOSS

Risk is limited to Strike B minus Strike A, minus the net credit received when establishing the position.

% MARGIN REQUIREMENT

See Appendix A for margin requirement.

✴ AS TIME GOES BY

For this play, time decay is your friend. Ideally you want all of the options in this spread to expire worthless.

📈 IMPLIED VOLATILITY

After the play is established, increasing implied volatility is the enemy. Your main concern is the at-the-money options you've sold. An increase in implied volatility will increase the prices of these options, so if you choose to close your position prior to expiration, it will be more expensive to buy them back.

In addition, you want the stock price to remain stable, but an increase in implied volatility suggests an increased possibility of a price swing.

✔ CHECK YOUR PLAY WITH TRADEKING TOOLS

• Use the Profit + Loss Calculator to establish break-even points, evaluate how your strategy might change as expiration approaches, and analyze the Greeks.

SPLIT STRIKE BUTTERFLY W/ CALLS

AKA Broken Wing Butterfly; Skip Strike Butterfly

THE SETUP

- Buy a call, Strike Price A
- Sell 2 calls, Strike Price B
- Skip over Strike Price C
- Buy a call, Strike Price D
- Generally, the stock will be at or below Strike A

NOTE: Strike prices are equidistant, and all options have the same expiration month.

WHO SHOULD RUN IT

Seasoned Veterans and higher

NOTE: Due to the narrow sweet spot and the fact you're trading four different options in one play, split strike butterflies may be better suited for more advanced option traders.

WHEN TO RUN IT

 You're slightly bullish. You want the stock to rise to Strike B and then stop.

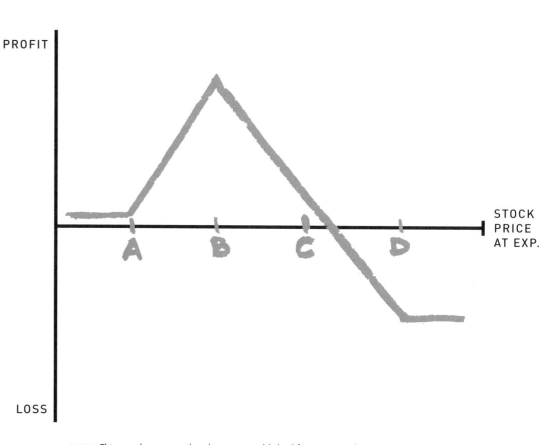

NOTE: This graph assumes the play was established for a net credit.

THE STRATEGY

You can think of this play as embedding a short call spread (Play Fourteen) inside a long butterfly spread with calls (Play Nineteen). Essentially, you're selling the short call spread to help pay for the butterfly. Because establishing those spreads separately would entail both buying and selling a call with Strike C, they cancel each other out and it becomes a dead strike.

The embedded short call spread makes it possible to establish this play for a net credit or a relatively small net debit. However, due to the addition of the short call spread, there is more risk than with a traditional butterfly.

A split-strike butterfly with calls is more of a directional play than a standard butterfly. Ideally, you want the stock price to increase somewhat, but not beyond Strike B. In this case, the calls with Strikes B and D will approach zero, but you'll retain the premium for the call with Strike A.

This play is usually run with the stock price at Strike A. That helps manage the risk, because the stock will have to make a significant move upward before you encounter the maximum loss.

👤 OPTIONS GUY'S TIPS:

👉 Some investors may wish to run this play using index options rather than options on individual stocks. That's because historically, indexes have not been as volatile as individual stocks. Fluctuations in an index's component stock prices tend to cancel one another out, lessening the volatility of the index as a whole.

🔟 BREAK-EVEN AT EXPIRATION

If established for a net credit (as in the graph at left) then the break-even point is Strike C plus the net credit received when establishing the play.

If established for a net debit, then there are two break-even points:

• Strike A plus net debit paid.

• Strike C minus net debit paid.

💲 THE SWEET SPOT

You want the stock price to be exactly at Strike B at expiration.

⬆ MAXIMUM POTENTIAL PROFIT

Potential profit is limited to Strike B minus Strike A minus the net debit paid, or plus the net credit received.

⬇ MAXIMUM POTENTIAL LOSS

Risk is limited to the difference between Strike C and Strike D minus the net credit received or plus the net debit paid.

% MARGIN REQUIREMENT

See Appendix A for margin requirement.

⏱ AS TIME GOES BY

For this play, time decay is your friend. Ideally, you want all options except the call with Strike A to expire worthless.

⚡ IMPLIED VOLATILITY

After the play is established, increasing implied volatility is the enemy. Your main concern is the options you've sold with Strike B. An increase in implied volatility will increase the price of these options, so if you choose to close your position prior to expiration, it will be more expensive to buy them back.

In addition, you want the stock price to remain stable, but an increase in implied volatility suggests an increased possibility of a price swing.

✅ CHECK YOUR PLAY WITH TRADEKING TOOLS

• Use the Profit + Loss Calculator to establish break-even points, evaluate how your strategy might change as expiration approaches, and analyze the Greeks.

• When using this as a bullish play, use the Technical Analysis Tool to look for directional indicators.

SPLIT STRIKE BUTTERFLY W/ PUTS

AKA Broken Wing Butterfly; Skip Strike Butterfly

THE SETUP

- Buy a put, Strike Price A

- Skip Strike Price B

- Sell 2 puts, Strike Price C

- Buy a put, Strike Price D

- Generally, the stock will be at or above Strike D

NOTE: Strike prices are equidistant, and all options have the same expiration month.

WHO SHOULD RUN IT

Seasoned Veterans and higher

NOTE: Due to the narrow sweet spot and the fact you're trading four different options in one play, split strike butterflies may be better suited for more advanced option traders.

WHEN TO RUN IT

 You're slightly bearish. You want the stock to go down to Strike C and then stop.

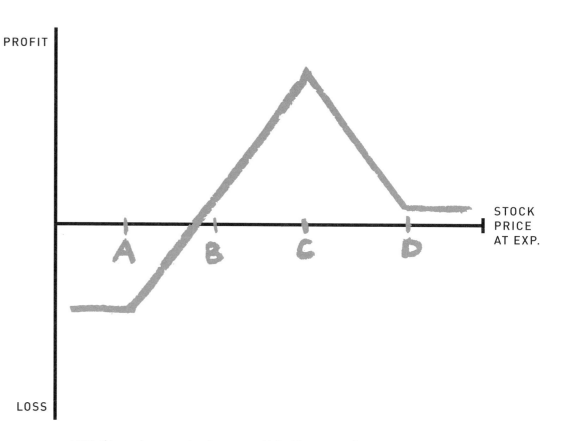

NOTE: This graph assumes the play was established for a net credit.

THE STRATEGY

You can think of this play as embedding a short put spread (Play Sixteen) inside a long butterfly spread with puts (Play Twenty). Essentially, you're selling the short put spread to help pay for the butterfly. Because establishing those spreads separately would entail both buying and selling a put with Strike B, they cancel each other out and it becomes a dead strike.

The embedded short put spread makes it possible to establish this play for a net credit or a relatively small net debit. However, due to the addition of the short put spread, there is more risk than with a traditional butterfly.

A split-strike butterfly is more of a directional play than a standard butterfly. Ideally, you want the stock price to decrease somewhat, but not beyond Strike C. In this case, the puts with Strikes A and C will approach zero, but you'll retain the premium for the put with Strike D.

This play is usually run with the stock price at Strike D. That helps manage the risk, because the stock will have to make a significant downward move before you encounter the maximum loss.

OPTIONS GUY'S TIPS:

☛ Some investors may wish to run this play using index options rather than options on individual stocks. That's because historically, indexes have not been as volatile as individual stocks. Fluctuations in an index's component stock prices tend to cancel one another out, lessening the volatility of the index as a whole.

⊙ BREAK-EVEN AT EXPIRATION

If established for a net credit (as in the graph at left) then the break-even point is Strike B minus the net credit received when establishing the play.

If established for a net debit, then there are two break-even points:

- Strike D minus net debit paid.
- Strike B plus net debit paid.

$ THE SWEET SPOT

You want the stock price to be exactly at Strike C at expiration.

⬆ MAXIMUM POTENTIAL PROFIT

Potential profit is limited to Strike D minus Strike C minus the net debit paid, or plus the net credit received.

⬇ MAXIMUM POTENTIAL LOSS

Risk is limited to the difference between Strike A and Strike B, minus the net credit received or plus the net debit paid.

% MARGIN REQUIREMENT

See Appendix A for margin requirement.

✪ AS TIME GOES BY

For this play, time decay is your friend. Ideally, you want all options except the put with Strike D to expire worthless.

⊕ IMPLIED VOLATILITY

After the play is established, increasing implied volatility is the enemy. Your main concern is the options you've sold with Strike C. An increase in implied volatility will increase the price of these options, so if you choose to close your position prior to expiration, it will be more expensive to buy them back.

In addition, you want the stock price to remain stable, but an increase in implied volatility suggests an increased possibility of a price swing.

✔ CHECK YOUR PLAY WITH TRADEKING TOOLS

- Use the Profit + Loss Calculator to establish break-even points, evaluate how your strategy might change as expiration approaches, and analyze the Greeks.

- When using this as a bearish play, use the Technical Analysis Tool to look for directional indicators.

LONG CONDOR SPREAD W/ CALLS

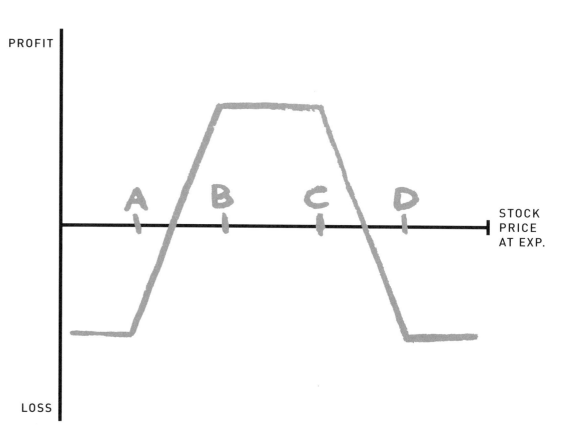

PROFIT

LOSS

STOCK PRICE AT EXP.

A B C D

THE SETUP

- Buy a call, Strike A
- Sell a call, Strike B
- Sell a call, Strike C
- Buy a call, Strike D
- Generally, the stock will be between Strike B and Strike C

NOTE: All options have the same expiration month.

WHO SHOULD RUN IT

Veterans or higher

WHEN TO RUN IT

(N) You're anticipating minimal movement on the stock within a specific time frame.

THE STRATEGY

You can think of a long condor spread with calls as simultaneously running an in-the-money long call spread (Play Thirteen) and an out-of-the-money short call spread (Play Fourteen). Ideally, you want the short call spread to expire worthless, while the long call spread achieves its maximum value with Strikes A and B in-the-money.

Typically, the stock will be halfway between Strike B and Strike C when you construct your spread. If the stock is not in the center at initiation, the play will be either bullish or bearish.

The distance between Strikes A and B is usually the same as the distance between Strikes C and D. However, the distance between Strikes B and C may vary to give you a wider sweet spot (see options guy tip).

You want the stock price to end up somewhere between Strike B and Strike C at expiration. Condor spreads have a wider sweet spot than the butterflies. But (as always) there's a tradeoff. In this case, it's that your potential profit is lower.

👤 OPTIONS GUY'S TIPS:

☞ You may wish to consider ensuring that Strike B and Strike C are one standard deviation or more away from the stock price at initiation. That will increase your probability of success. However, the further these strike prices are from the current stock price, the lower the potential profit will be from this play.

☞ Some investors may wish to run this play using index options rather than options on individual stocks. That's because historically, indexes have not been as volatile as individual stocks. Fluctuations in an index's component stock prices tend to cancel one another out, lessening the volatility of the index as a whole.

☞ As a general rule of thumb, you may wish to consider running this play approximately 30-45 days from expiration to take advantage of accelerating time decay as expiration approaches. Of course, this depends on the underlying stock and market conditions such as implied volatility.

🔟 BREAK-EVEN AT EXPIRATION

There are two break-even points:

- Strike A plus the net debit paid.

- Strike D minus the net debit paid.

💲 THE SWEET SPOT

You achieve maximum profit if the stock price is anywhere between Strike B and Strike C at expiration.

⬆ MAXIMUM POTENTIAL PROFIT

Potential profit is limited to Strike B minus Strike A minus the net debit paid.

⬇ MAXIMUM POTENTIAL LOSS

Risk is limited to the net debit paid to establish the condor.

％ MARGIN REQUIREMENT

After the trade is paid for, no additional margin is required.

⌛ AS TIME GOES BY

For this play, time decay is your friend. Ideally, you want the options with Strike C and Strike D to expire worthless, and the options with Strike A and Strike B to retain their intrinsic values.

⚡ IMPLIED VOLATILITY

After the play is established, increasing implied volatility is the enemy. Your main concern is the options you've sold with Strikes B and C. An increase in implied volatility will increase the prices of these options, so if you choose to close your position prior to expiration, it will be more expensive to buy them back.

In addition, you want the stock price to remain stable, but an increase in implied volatility suggests an increased possibility of a price swing.

✅ CHECK YOUR PLAY WITH TRADEKING TOOLS

- Use the Profit + Loss Calculator to establish break-even points, evaluate how your strategy might change as expiration approaches, and analyze the Greeks.

- Use the Probability Calculator to verify that Strikes B and Strike C are approximately one standard deviation (or more) away from the stock price. (See Options Guy's Tips for more information.)

LONG CONDOR SPREAD W/ PUTS

THE SETUP

- Buy a put, Strike A
- Sell a put, Strike B
- Sell a put, Strike C
- Buy a put, Strike D
- Generally, the stock will be between Strike B and Strike C

NOTE: All options have the same expiration month.

WHO SHOULD RUN IT

Veterans or higher

WHEN TO RUN IT

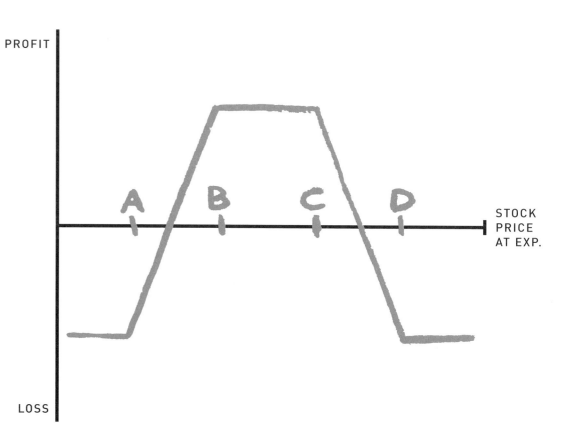

(N) You're anticipating minimal movement on the stock within a specific time frame.

THE STRATEGY

You can think of long condor spread with puts as simultaneously running an in-the-money short put spread (Play Sixteen) and an out-of-the-money long put spread (Play Fifteen). Ideally, you want the short put spread to expire worthless, while the long put spread achieves its maximum value with Strikes C and D in-the-money.

Typically, the stock will be halfway between Strike B and Strike C when you construct your spread. If the stock is not in the center at initiation, the play will be either bullish or bearish.

The distance between Strikes A and B is usually the same as the distance between Strikes C and D. However, the distance between Strikes B and C may vary to give you a wider sweet spot (see options guy tip).

You want the stock price to end up somewhere between Strike B and Strike C at expiration. Condor spreads have a wider sweet spot than the butterflies. But (as always) there's a tradeoff. In this case, it's that your potential profit is lower.

OPTIONS GUY'S TIPS:

☞ You may wish to consider ensuring that Strike B and Strike C are one standard deviation or more away from the stock price at initiation. That will increase your probability of success. However, the further these Strike Prices are from the current stock price, the lower the potential profit will be from this play.

☞ Some investors may wish to run this play using index options rather than options on individual stocks. That's because historically, indexes have not been as volatile as individual stocks. Fluctuations in an index's component stock prices tend to cancel one another out, lessening the volatility of the index as a whole.

☞ As a general rule of thumb, you may wish to consider running this play approximately 30-45 days from expiration to take advantage of accelerating time decay as expiration approaches. Of course, this depends on the underlying stock and market conditions such as implied volatility.

BREAK-EVEN AT EXPIRATION

There are two break-even points:

- Strike A plus the net debit paid.
- Strike D minus the net debit paid.

THE SWEET SPOT

You achieve maximum profit if the stock price is anywhere between Strike B and Strike C at expiration.

MAXIMUM POTENTIAL PROFIT

Potential profit is limited to Strike D minus Strike C minus the net debit paid.

MAXIMUM POTENTIAL LOSS

Risk is limited to the net debit paid to establish the condor.

MARGIN REQUIREMENT

After the trade is paid for, no additional margin is required.

AS TIME GOES BY

For this play, time decay is your friend. Ideally, you want the options with Strike A and Strike B to expire worthless, and the options with Strike C and Strike D to retain their intrinsic values.

IMPLIED VOLATILITY

After the play is established, increasing implied volatility is the enemy. Your main concern is the options you've sold with Strikes B and C. An increase in implied volatility will increase the prices of these options, so if you choose to close your position prior to expiration, it will be more expensive to buy them back.

In addition, you want the stock price to remain stable, but an increase in implied volatility suggests an increased possibility of a price swing.

CHECK YOUR PLAY WITH TRADEKING TOOLS

- Use the Profit + Loss Calculator to establish break-even points, evaluate how your strategy might change as expiration approaches, and analyze the Greeks.

- Use the Probability Calculator to verify that Strikes B and Strike C are approximately one standard deviation (or more) away from the stock price. (See Options Guy's Tips for more information.)

LONG IRON CONDOR

THE SETUP

- Buy a put, Strike A

- Sell a put, Strike B

- Sell a call, Strike C

- Buy a call, Strike D

- Generally, the stock will be between Strike B and Strike C

NOTE: All options have the same expiration month.

WHO SHOULD RUN IT

Veterans or higher

WHEN TO RUN IT

(N) You're anticipating minimal movement on the stock within a specific time frame.

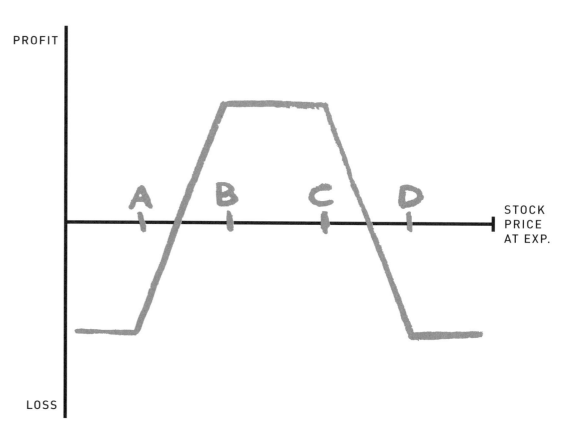

THE STRATEGY

You can think of this play as simultaneously running an out-of-the-money short put spread (Play Sixteen) and an out-of-the-money short call spread (Play Fourteen). Some investors consider this to be a more attractive strategy than a long condor spread with calls or puts because you receive a net credit into your account right off the bat.

Typically, the stock will be halfway between Strike B and Strike C when you construct your spread. If the stock is not in the center at initiation, the play will be either bullish or bearish.

The distance between Strikes A and B is usually the same as the distance between Strikes C and D. However, the distance between Strikes B and C may vary to give you a wider sweet spot (see options guy tip).

You want the stock price to end up somewhere between Strike B and Strike C at expiration. A Long Iron Condor spread has a wider sweet spot than a Long Iron Butterfly. But (as always) there's a tradeoff. In this case, it's that your potential profit is lower.

👤 OPTIONS GUY'S TIPS:

☞ One advantage of this strategy is that you want all of the options to expire worthless. If that happens, you won't have to pay any commissions to get out of your position.

☞ You may wish to consider ensuring that Strike B and Strike C are one standard deviation or more away from the stock price at initiation. That will increase your probability of success. However, the further these Strike Prices are from the current stock price, the lower the potential profit will be from this play.

☞ As a general rule of thumb, you may wish to consider running this play approximately 30-45 days from expiration to take advantage of accelerating time decay as expiration approaches. Of course, this depends on the underlying stock and market conditions such as implied volatility.

☞ Some investors may wish to run this play using index options rather than options on individual stocks. That's because historically, indexes have not been as volatile as individual stocks. Fluctuations in an index's component stock prices tend to cancel one another out, lessening the volatility of the index as a whole.

🔟 BREAK-EVEN AT EXPIRATION

There are two break-even points:

• Strike B minus the net credit received.

• Strike C plus the net credit received.

💲 THE SWEET SPOT

You achieve maximum profit if the stock price is between Strike B and Strike C at expiration.

⬆ MAXIMUM POTENTIAL PROFIT

Profit is limited to the net credit received.

⬇ MAXIMUM POTENTIAL LOSS

Risk is limited to Strike B minus Strike A, minus the net credit received.

% MARGIN REQUIREMENT

See Appendix A for margin requirement.

☽ AS TIME GOES BY

For this play, time decay is your friend. You want all four options to expire worthless.

⊕ IMPLIED VOLATILITY

After the play is established, increasing implied volatility is the enemy. Your main concern is the options you've sold with Strikes B and C. An increase in implied volatility will increase the prices of these options, so if you choose to close your position prior to expiration, it will be more expensive to buy them back.

In addition, you want the stock price to remain stable, but an increase in implied volatility suggests an increased possibility of a price swing.

✔ CHECK YOUR PLAY WITH TRADEKING TOOLS

• Use the Profit + Loss Calculator to establish break-even points, evaluate how your strategy might change as expiration approaches, and analyze the Greeks.

• Use the Probability Calculator to verify that Strikes B and Strike C are approximately one standard deviation (or more) away from the stock price. (See Options Guy's Tips for more information.)

LONG CALENDAR SPREAD W/ CALLS

AKA Time Spread; Horizontal Spread

THE SETUP

• Sell a call, Strike Price A
(near-term expiration – "front-month")

• Buy a call, Strike Price A
(with expiration one month later – "back-month")

• Generally, the stock will be at Strike A

WHO SHOULD RUN IT

Seasoned Veterans and higher

NOTE: The level of knowledge required for this trade is considerable, because you're dealing with options that expire on different dates.

WHEN TO RUN IT

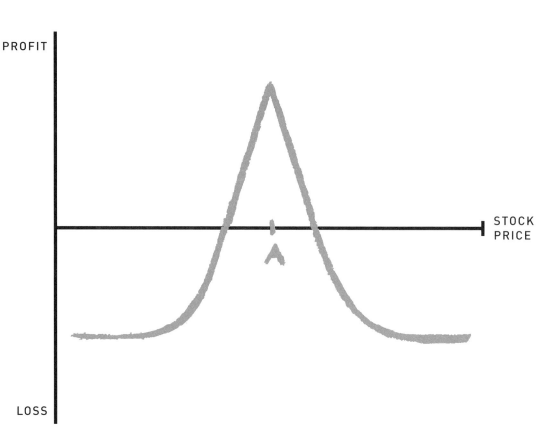

(N) You're anticipating minimal movement on the stock within a specific time frame.

Notice the profit and loss lines are not straight. That's because the back-month call is still open when the front-month call expires. Straight lines and hard angles usually indicate that all options in the play have the same expiration date.

THE STRATEGY

When running a calendar spread with calls, you're selling and buying a call with the same Strike Price, but the call you buy will have a later expiration date than the call you sell. You're taking advantage of accelerating time decay on the front-month (shorter-term) call as expiration approaches. Just before front-month expiration, you want to buy back the shorter-term call for next to nothing. At the same time, you will sell the back-month call to close your position. Ideally, the back-month call will still have significant time value.

If you're anticipating minimal movement on the stock, construct your calendar spread with at-the-money calls. If you're mildly bullish, use slightly out-of-the-money calls. This can give you a lower up-front cost.

Because the front-month and back-month options both have the same strike price, you cannot capture any intrinsic value on the options. You can only capture time value. However, as the calls get deep in-the-money or far out-of-the-money, time value will begin to disappear. Time premium is maximized with at-the-money options, so you need the stock price to stay as close to Strike A as possible.

For the purpose of this playbook, we're using the example of a one-month calendar spread. But please note, it is possible to use different time intervals. If you're going to use more than a one-month interval between the front-month and back-month options, you need to understand the ins and outs of "rolling." (See the "How We Roll" section of this book.)

OPTIONS GUY'S TIPS:

When establishing one-month calendar spreads, you may wish to consider a "risk one to make two" philosophy. That is, for every net debit of $1 at initiation, you're hoping to receive $2 when closing the position. Use TradeKing's Profit + Loss Calculator to estimate whether this seems possible.

BREAK-EVEN AT EXPIRATION

It is possible to approximate break-even points, but there are too many variables to give an exact formula.

Because there are two expiration dates for the options in a calendar spread, a pricing model must be used to "guesstimate" what the value of the back-month call will be when the front-month call expires. TradeKing's Profit + Loss Calculator can help you in this regard. But keep in mind, the Profit + Loss Calculator assumes that all other variables, such as implied volatility, interest rates, etc., remain constant over the life of the trade – and they may not behave that way in reality.

THE SWEET SPOT

You want the stock price to be at Strike A when the front-month option expires.

MAXIMUM POTENTIAL PROFIT

Potential profit is limited to the premium received for the back-month call minus the cost to buy back the front-month call, minus the net debit paid to establish the position.

MAXIMUM POTENTIAL LOSS

Limited to the net debit paid to establish the trade (if the entire position is closed prior to front-month expiration).

MARGIN REQUIREMENT

After the trade is paid for, no additional margin is required if the position is closed at expiration of the front-month option.

AS TIME GOES BY

For this play, time decay is your friend. Because time decay accelerates close to expiration, the front-month call will lose value faster than the back-month call.

CONTINUED **ON NEXT PAGE**

CONTINUED FROM CALENDAR SPREAD W/ CALLS

⊕ IMPLIED VOLATILITY

For this play, although you don't want the stock to move much, you're better off if implied volatility increases close to front-month expiration. That will cause the back-month call price to increase, while having little effect on the price of the front-month option. (Near expiration, there is hardly any time value for implied volatility to mess with.)

✔ CHECK YOUR PLAY WITH TRADEKING TOOLS

• Use the Profit + Loss Calculator to estimate break-even points, evaluate how your strategy might change as expiration approaches, and analyze the Greeks.

• Use the Profit + Loss Calculator to estimate profit potential by determining what the back-month option will be trading for at the expiration of the front month.

LONG CALENDAR SPREAD W/ PUTS

AKA Time Spread, Horizontal Spread

THE SETUP

• Sell a put, Strike Price A
(near-term expiration – "front-month")

• Buy a put, Strike Price A
(with expiration one month later – "back-month")

• Generally, the stock will be at Strike A

WHO SHOULD RUN IT

Seasoned Veterans and higher

NOTE: The level of knowledge required for this trade is considerable, because you're dealing with options that expire on different dates.

WHEN TO RUN IT

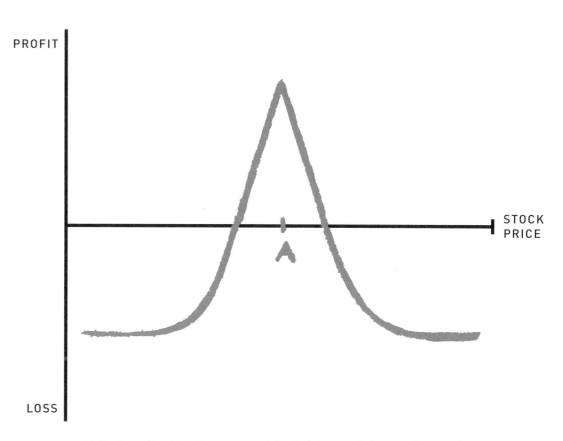

N You're anticipating minimal movement on the stock within a specific time frame.

Notice the profit and loss lines are not straight. That's because the front-month put is still open when the back-month put expires. Straight lines and hard angles usually indicate that all options in the play have the same expiration date.

CONTINUED FROM CALENDAR SPREAD W/ PUTS

THE STRATEGY

When running a calendar spread with puts, you're selling and buying a put with the same Strike Price, but the put you buy will have a later expiration date than the put you sell. You're taking advantage of accelerating time decay on the front-month (shorter-term) put as expiration approaches. Just before front-month expiration, you want to buy back the shorter-term put for next to nothing. At the same time, you will sell the back-month put to close your position. Ideally, the back-month put will still have significant time value.

If you're anticipating minimal movement on the stock, construct your calendar spread with at-the-money puts. If you're mildly bearish, use slightly out-of-the-money puts. This can give you a lower up-front cost.

Because the front-month and back-month options both have the same strike price, you cannot capture any intrinsic value. You can only capture time value. However, as the puts get deep in-the-money or far out-of-the-money, time value will begin to disappear. Time premium is maximized with at-the-money options, so you need the stock price to stay as close to Strike A as possible.

For the purpose of this playbook, we're using the example of a one-month calendar spread. But please note, it is possible to use different time intervals. If you're going to use more than a one-month interval between the front-month and back-month options, you need to understand the ins and outs of "rolling." (See the "How We Roll" section of this book.)

👤 OPTIONS GUY'S TIPS:

☞ When establishing one-month calendar spreads, you may wish to consider a "risk one to make two" philosophy. That is, for every net debit of $1 at initiation, you're hoping to receive $2 when closing the position. Use the TradeKing's Profit + Loss Calculator to estimate whether this seems possible.

🄾 BREAK-EVEN POINT

It is possible to approximate break-even points, but there are too many variables to give an exact formula.

Because there are two expiration dates for the options in a calendar spread, a pricing model must be used to "guesstimate" what the value of the back-month put will be when the front-month put expires. TradeKing's Profit + Loss Calculator can help you in this regard. But keep in mind, the Profit + Loss Calculator assumes that all other variables, such as implied volatility, interest rates, etc., remain constant over the life of the trade – and they may not behave that way in reality.

💲 THE SWEET SPOT

You want the stock price to be at Strike A when the front-month option expires.

⬆ MAXIMUM POTENTIAL PROFIT

Potential profit is limited to the premium received for the back-month put minus the cost to buy back the front-month put, minus the net debit paid to establish the position.

⬇ MAXIMUM POTENTIAL LOSS

Limited to the net debit paid to establish the trade (if the entire position is closed prior to front-month expiration).

% MARGIN REQUIREMENT

After the trade is paid for, no additional margin is required if the position is closed at expiration of the front-month option.

⏱ AS TIME GOES BY

For this play, time decay is your friend. Because time decay accelerates close to expiration, the front-month put will lose value faster than the back-month put.

CONTINUED ON NEXT PAGE

⊕ IMPLIED VOLATILITY

For this play, although you don't want the stock to move much, you're better off if implied volatility increases close to front-month expiration. That will cause the back-month put price to increase, while having little effect on the price of the front-month option. (Near expiration, there is hardly any time value for implied volatility to mess with.)

✓ CHECK YOUR PLAY WITH TRADEKING TOOLS

• Use the Profit + Loss Calculator to estimate break-even points, evaluate how your strategy might change as expiration approaches, and analyze the Greeks.

• Use the Profit + Loss Calculator to estimate profit potential by determining what the back-month option will be trading for at the expiration of the front month.

DIAGONAL SPREAD W/ CALLS

THE SETUP

• Sell an out-of-the-money call, Strike Price A (near-term expiration – "front-month")

• Buy a further out-of-the-money call, Strike Price B (with expiration one month later – "back-month")

• At expiration of the front-month call, sell another call with Strike A and the same expiration as the back-month call

• Generally, the stock will be below Strike A

WHO SHOULD RUN IT

Seasoned Veterans and higher

NOTE: The level of knowledge required for this trade is considerable, because you're dealing with options that expire on different dates.

WHEN TO RUN IT

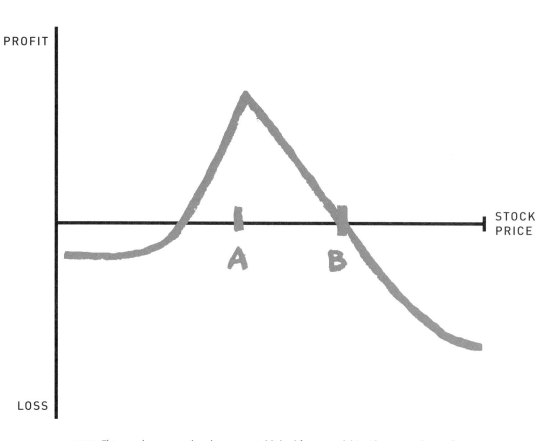

You're expecting neutral activity during the front month, then neutral to bearish activity during the back month.

NOTE: This graph assumes the play was established for a net debit. Also notice the profit and loss lines are not straight. That's because the front-month put is still open when the back-month put expires. Straight lines and hard angles usually indicate that all options in the play have the same expiration date.

THE STRATEGY

You can think of this as a two-step play. It's a combination of a long calendar spread with calls (Play Twenty-Seven) and a short call spread (Play Fourteen). It starts out as a time decay play. Then once you sell a second call with Strike A (after front-month expiration) you have legged into a short call spread. Ideally, you will be able to establish this play for a net credit or for a small net debit. Then, the sale of the second call will be all gravy.

For the purpose of this playbook, we're using the example of one-month diagonal spreads. But please note, it is possible to use different time intervals. If you're going to use more than a one-month interval between the front-month and back-month options, you need to understand the ins and outs of "rolling." (See the "How We Roll" section of this book.)

👤 OPTIONS GUY'S TIPS:

☞ Ideally, you want some initial volatility with some predictability. Some volatility is good, because the plan is to sell two options and you want to get as much as possible for them. On the other hand, we want the stock price to remain relatively stable. That's a bit of a paradox, and that's why this play is for more advanced traders.

🔟 BREAK-EVEN POINTS

It is possible to approximate break-even points, but there are too many variables to give an exact formula.

Because there are two expiration dates for the options in a diagonal spread, a pricing model must be used to "guesstimate" what the value of the back-month call will be when the front-month call expires. TradeKing's Profit + Loss Calculator can help you in this regard. But keep in mind, the Profit + Loss Calculator assumes that all other variables, such as implied volatility, interest rates, etc. remain constant over the life of the trade – and they may not behave in reality.

💲 THE SWEET SPOT

For step one, you want the stock price to stay at or around Strike A until expiration of the front-month option. For step two, you'll want the stock price to be below Strike A when the back-month option expires.

⬆ MAXIMUM POTENTIAL PROFIT*

Potential profit is limited to the net credit received for selling both calls with Strike A, minus the premium paid for the call with Strike B.

*You can not precisely calculate potential profit at initiation, because it depends on the premium received for the sale of the second call at a later date.

⬇ MAXIMUM POTENTIAL LOSS*

If established for a net credit, risk is limited to the difference between Strike A and Strike B, minus the net credit received.

If established for a net debit, risk is limited to the difference between Strike A and Strike B, plus the net debit paid.

* You can not precisely calculate your risk at initiation of this play, because it depends on the premium received for the sale of the second call at a later date.

％ MARGIN REQUIREMENT

See Appendix A for margin requirement.

❇ AS TIME GOES BY

For this play, before front-month expiration, time decay is your friend, since the shorter-term call will lose time value faster than the longer-term call. After closing the front-month call with Strike A and selling another call with Strike A that has the same expiration as the back-month call with Strike B, time decay is somewhat neutral. That's because you'll see erosion in the value of both the option you sold (good) and the option you bought (bad).

CONTINUED **ON NEXT PAGE**

◆ IMPLIED VOLATILITY

For this play, although you want neutral movement on the stock, you're better off if implied volatility increases close to front-month expiration. That way, you will receive a higher premium for selling another call with Strike A.

After expiration of the front-month call, the net effect of an increase in implied volatility is somewhat neutral. The option you sold will increase in value (bad), but it will also increase the value of the option you bought (good).

✔ CHECK YOUR PLAY WITH TRADEKING TOOLS

• Use the Profit + Loss Calculator to estimate break-even points, evaluate how your strategy might change as expiration approaches, and analyze the Greeks.

• Use the Option Pricing Calculator to "guesstimate" the value of the back-month call you will sell with Strike A after closing the front-month call.

DIAGONAL SPREAD W/ PUTS

THE SETUP

• Sell an out-of-the-money put, Strike Price B (Near-term expiration – "front-month")

• Buy a further out-of-the-money put, Strike Price A (With expiration one month later – "back-month")

• At expiration of the front-month put, sell another put with Strike B and the same expiration as the back-month put

• Generally, the stock will be above Strike B

WHO SHOULD RUN IT

Seasoned Veterans and higher

NOTE: The level of knowledge required for this trade is considerable, because you're dealing with options that expire on different dates.

WHEN TO RUN IT

(N) (bull) You're expecting neutral activity during the front month, then neutral to bullish activity during the back month.

NOTE: This graph assumes the play was established for a net debit. Also notice the profit and loss lines are not straight. That's because the front-month put is still open when the back-month put expires. Straight lines and hard angles usually indicate that all options in the play have the same expiration date.

THE STRATEGY

You can think of this as a two-step play. It's a combination of a long calendar spread with puts (Play Twenty-Eight) and a short put spread (Play Sixteen). It starts out as a time decay play. Then once you sell a second put with Strike B (after front-month expiration), you have legged into a short put spread. Ideally, you will be able to establish this play for a net credit or for a small net debit.

For the purpose of this playbook, we're using the example of one-month diagonal spreads. But please note, it is possible to use different time intervals. If you're going to use more than a one-month interval between the front-month and back-month options, you need to understand the ins and outs of "rolling." (See the "How We Roll" section of this book.)

🧑 OPTIONS GUY'S TIPS:

☞ Ideally, you want some initial volatility with some predictability. Some volatility is good, because the plan is to sell two options and you want to get as much as possible for them. On the other hand, we want the stock price to remain relatively stable. That's a bit of a paradox, and that's why this play is for more advanced traders.

🔟 BREAK-EVEN POINTS

It is possible to approximate break-even points, but there are too many variables to give an exact formula.

Because there are two expiration dates for the options in a diagonal spread, a pricing model must be used to "guesstimate" what the value of the back-month put will be when the front-month put expires. TradeKing's Profit + Loss Calculator can help you in this regard. But keep in mind, the Profit + Loss Calculator assumes that all other variables, such as implied volatility, interest rates, etc., remain constant over the life of the trade – and they may not behave in reality.

💲 THE SWEET SPOT

For step one, you want the stock price to stay at or around Strike B until expiration of the front-month option. For step two, you'll want the stock price to be above Strike B when the back-month option expires.

⬆ MAXIMUM POTENTIAL PROFIT*

Profit is limited to the net credit received for selling both puts with Strike B, minus the premium paid for the put with Strike A.

*You can not precisely calculate potential profit at initiation, because it depends on the premium received for the sale of the second call at a later date.

⬇ MAXIMUM POTENTIAL LOSS*

If established for a net credit, risk is limited to the difference between Strike A and Strike B, minus the net credit received.

If established for a net debit, risk is limited to the difference between Strike A and Strike B, plus the net debit paid.

* You can not precisely calculate your risk at initiation of this play, because it depends on the premium received for the sale of the second put at a later date.

％ MARGIN REQUIREMENT

See Appendix A for margin requirement.

🕐 AS TIME GOES BY

For this play, before front-month expiration, time decay is your friend, since the shorter-term put will lose time value faster than the longer-term put. After closing the front-month put with Strike B and selling another put with Strike B that has the same expiration as the back-month put with Strike A, time decay is somewhat neutral. That's because you'll see erosion in the value of both the option you sold (good) and the option you bought (bad).

CONTINUED ON NEXT PAGE

⊕ IMPLIED VOLATILITY

For this play, although you want neutral movement on the stock, you're better off if implied volatility increases close to front-month expiration. That way, you will receive a higher premium for selling another put with Strike B.

After expiration of the front-month call, the net effect of an increase in implied volatility is somewhat neutral. The option you sold will increase in value (bad), but it will also increase the value of the option you bought (good).

✓ CHECK YOUR PLAY WITH TRADEKING TOOLS

• Use the Profit + Loss Calculator to estimate break-even points, evaluate how your strategy might change as expiration approaches, and analyze the Greeks.

• Use the Option Pricing Calculator to "guesstimate" the value of the back-month call you will sell at Strike B after closing the front-month put.

FINAL

THOUGHTS

HOW WE ROLL

AN INTRODUCTION TO THE CONCEPT OF "ROLLING"

Rolling is one of the most common ways to adjust an option position. It's possible to roll either a long or short option position, but in this section, we're going to focus on the short side.

When you roll a short position, you're buying to close an existing position and selling to open a new one. You're tweaking the strike prices on your options, and/or "rolling" the expiration further out in time.

When you decide to roll, you've changed your opinion on the underlying stock. So rolling is a way of trying to put off assignment, or even avoid it altogether. It's an advanced technique, and it's one you need to thoroughly understand before executing. When rolling, it is possible to compound your losses. So exercise caution, and don't get greedy.

This section is meant to be an introduction to how rolling works, so the examples we present are somewhat simplified. They're merely designed to familiarize you with this concept – not instruct you how to roll more complicated strategies like spreads.

To help you grasp this concept, we'll examine the process of rolling two basic positions: a covered call and a cash-secured put.

You might notice we use some lingo in this section that we didn't use very much throughout the rest of the book. It's safe to assume if you don't thoroughly understand the terminology, you should learn more about options before attempting this maneuver.

ROLLING A COVERED CALL

Imagine you're running a 30-day covered call (Play Six) on stock XYZ with a strike price of $90. That means you own 100 shares of XYZ stock, and you've sold one 90-Strike call a month from expiration. When you sold the call, the stock price was $87.50, and you received a premium of $1.30, or $130 total since one contract equals 100 shares. Now, with expiration fast approaching, the stock has gone up to $92. In all probability you will be assigned and have to sell the stock at $90.

The only way to avoid assignment for sure is to buy back the 90-Strike call before it is assigned, and cancel your obligation. However, the 90-Strike call is now trading for $2.10, so it will hurt a bit to buy it back. To help offset the cost of buying back the call, we're going to "roll up and out."

That means you want to go "up" in strike price and "out" in time. The idea is to balance the decrease in premium for selling a higher OTM strike price vs. the greater premium you'll receive for selling an option that is further from expiration (and thus, has more "time value"). Here's an example of how that might work.

Using TradeKing's spread order screen, you enter a buy to close order for the front-month 90-Strike call. In the same trade, you sell to open an OTM 95-Strike call (rolling up) that's 60 days from expiration (rolling out). Due to higher time premium, the back-month 95-Strike call will be trading for $2.30. Since you're paying $2.10 to buy back the front-month call and receiving $2.30 for the back-month call, this trade can be accomplished for a net credit of $0.20 ($2.30 sale price - $2.10 purchase price) or $20 total.

Let's look at all the good news and bad news surrounding this trade. As you'll see, it's a double-edged sword.

Since you've raised the strike price to $95, you have more profit potential on the stock. The obligation to sell was at $90, but now it's at $95. The bad news is, you had to buy back the front-month call for 80 cents more than you received when selling it ($2.10 paid to close - $1.30 received to open). On the other hand, you've more than covered the cost of buying it back by selling the back-month 95-Strike call for more premium. So that's good.

But you have to consider the fact that there are still 60 days before the new options expire, and you don't really know what will happen with the stock during that time. You'll just have to keep your fingers crossed and hope for the best.

If the back-month 95-Strike short call expires worthless when all's said and done in 60 days, you wind up with a $1.50 net credit. Here's the math: You lost a total of $0.80 after buying back the 90-Strike front-month call. However, you received a premium of $2.30 for the 95-Strike call, so you netted $1.50 ($2.30 back-month premium - $0.80 front-month loss) or $150 total. That's not a bad outcome. (See Ex.1)

However, if the market makes a big move upward in the next 60 days, you might be tempted to roll up and out again. But beware.

EX. 1: ROLLING A CALL UP AND OUT

Existing Position: 30-day 90-strike call Premium received	+$1.30
Premium paid to close 90-Strike call	-$2.10
Premium received to open 60-day 95-Strike call	+$2.30
Net credit from the roll	+$0.20

$1.30 initial premium + $0.20 net credit from roll
= **+$1.50 net total** from this series of trades.

EX. 2: ROLLING A PUT DOWN AND OUT

Existing Position: 30-day 50-Strike put Premium received	+$0.90
Premium paid to close 50-Strike put	-$1.55
Premium received to open 90-day 47.50-Strike put	+$1.70
Net credit from the roll	+$0.15

$0.90 initial premium + $0.15 net credit from roll
= **+$1.05 net total** from this series of trades.

Every time you roll up and out, you may be taking a loss on the front-month call. Furthermore, you still have not secured any gains on the back-month call or on the stock appreciation, because the market still has time to move against you. And that means you could wind up compounding your losses. So come to think of it, rolling's not really a double-edged sword. It's more like a quadruple-edged shaving razor.

ROLLING A CASH-SECURED PUT

To avoid assignment on a short put, the roll here is "down and out."

For example, let's say you've sold a 30-day cash-secured put (Play Five) on stock XYZ with a strike price of $50. And let's say you received $0.90 for the put when the stock was trading at $51. Now, close to expiration, the stock has dropped and it's trading at $48.50.

The only way to avoid assignment for sure is to buy back the front-month 50-Strike put before it is assigned, and cancel your obligation. The problem is, the front-month put you originally sold for $0.90 is now trading at $1.55. Here's how you roll.

Using TradeKing's spread order screen, you enter a buy to close order for the front-month 50-Strike put. In the same trade, you sell to open a back-month 47.50-Strike put (rolling down), 90 days from expiration (rolling out) which is trading for $1.70. By doing this, you'll receive a net credit of $0.15 ($1.70 back-month sale price - $1.55 front-month purchase price) or $15 total.

You were able to roll for a net credit even though the back-month put is further OTM because of

the considerable increase in time premium of the 90-day option.

If the 47.50-Strike put expires worthless, when all is said and done in 90 days, you'll net $1.05. Here's the math: You lost a total of $0.65 on the front-month put ($1.55 paid to close - $0.90 received to open). However, you received a premium of $1.70 for the $47.50 -Strike put, so you netted $1.05 ($1.70 back month premium - $0.65 front-month loss) or $105 total. (See Ex. 2)

However, every time you roll down and out, you may be taking a loss on the front-month put. Furthermore, you have not secured any gains on the back-month put because the market still has time to move against you. And that means you could wind up compounding your losses.

OPTIONS GUY'S TIPS:

☞ You should usually roll out the shortest possible time period. That way, you will be faced with less market uncertainty. You may even wish to consider paying a small net debit for the roll to obtain the shorter time period.

☞ As an option you've sold gets in-the-money, you'll have to quickly decide whether or not you're going to roll. As a general rule of thumb, you should consider rolling before options you've sold get anywhere from 2-4% ITM, depending on the value of the stock and market conditions (e.g., implied volatility). If the option gets too deep ITM, it will be tough to roll for an acceptable net debit, never mind receiving a net credit.

☞ You may want to consider a "pre-emptive roll." That is, you can roll before the option gets ITM if you think it's headed that way. This might lower the cost of buying back the front-month option, and could result in a larger net credit for the roll.

APPENDIX A: MARGIN REQUIREMENTS

When running some of the option plays in this book, you need to keep cash in your account in case the trade goes against you. So we've indicated the initial margin for plays that have any requirement beyond the cost to establish the trade.

After the position is established, ongoing maintenance margin requirements may apply. That means depending how your options perform, an increase (or decrease) in the required margin is possible.

Keep in mind these requirements are subject to change. Furthermore, they're listed on a per-contract basis. So don't forget to multiply by the correct number of contracts when you're doing the math.

If you have any questions about your margin requirements, feel free to talk with TradeKing Customer Service at (877) 495-KING.

SHORT CALL

Margin requirement is the greater of the following:

25% of the underlying security value minus the out-of-the-money amount (if any), plus the premium received.

OR

10% of the underlying security value plus the premium received.

NOTE: The premium received from establishing the short call(s) may be applied to the initial margin requirement.

SHORT PUT

Margin requirement is the greater of the following:

25% of underlying security value minus the out-of-the-money amount (if any), plus the premium received.

OR

10% of the strike price of the put option plus the premium received.

NOTE: The premium received from establishing the short put(s) may be applied to the initial margin requirement.

CASH-SECURED PUT

You must have enough cash to cover the cost of purchasing the stock at the strike price.

NOTE: The premium received from establishing the short put(s) may be applied to the initial margin requirement.

SHORT STRADDLE

Margin requirement is the short call(s) or short put(s) requirement (whichever is greater), plus the premium received from the other side.

NOTE: The net credit received from establishing the short straddle may be applied to initial margin requirement.

SHORT STRANGLE

Margin requirement is the short call(s) or short put(s) requirement (whichever is greater), plus the credit received from the other side.

NOTE: The net credit received from establishing the short strangle may be applied to the initial margin requirement.

SHORT CALL SPREAD

Margin requirement is the lesser of the following:

The difference between strikes.

OR

The margin requirement for the short call position.

NOTE: The net credit received when establishing the short call spread may be applied to the initial margin requirement.

SHORT PUT SPREAD

Margin requirement is the lesser of the following:

The difference between strikes.

OR

The margin requirement for the short put position.

NOTE: The net credit received when establishing the short put spread may be applied to the initial margin requirement.

RATIO VERTICAL SPREAD WITH CALLS

Margin requirement is equal to the requirement for the uncovered short call(s) portion of the ratio vertical spread.

NOTE: If established for a net credit, the proceeds may be applied to the initial margin requirement.

RATIO VERTICAL SPREAD WITH PUTS

Margin requirement is equal to the requirement for the uncovered short put(s) portion of the ratio vertical spread.

NOTE: If established for a net credit, the proceeds may be applied to the initial margin requirement.

LONG IRON BUTTERFLY

Margin requirement is the greater of the following:

The short call spread requirement.

OR

The short put spread requirement.

NOTE: The net credit received when establishing the long iron butterfly may be applied to the initial margin requirement.

LONG IRON CONDOR

Margin requirement is the greater of the following:

The short call spread requirement.

OR

The short put spread requirement.

NOTE: The net credit received when establishing the long iron condor may be applied to the initial margin requirement.

SPLIT STRIKE BUTTERFLY WITH CALLS

Margin requirement is the exposure of the short call spread embedded into this strategy, minus the net credit (if any) or plus the net debit paid. (See the "Maximum Potential Loss" section of Play Twenty-Two on p. 75.)

SPLIT STRIKE BUTTERFLY WITH PUTS

Margin requirement is the exposure of the short put spread embedded into this strategy, minus the net credit (if any) or plus the net debit paid. (See the "Maximum Potential Loss" section of Play Twenty-Three on p. 77.)

DIAGONAL SPREAD WITH CALLS

Margin requirement is the difference between the strike prices, minus the net credit received or plus the net debit paid.*

* If the position is closed at expiration of the front-month option.

DIAGONAL SPREAD WITH PUTS

Margin requirement is the difference between the strike prices, minus the net credit received or plus the net debit paid.*

* If the position is closed at expiration of the front-month option.

**CONGRATULATIONS ON MAKING
IT ALL THE WAY TO THE END OF
THE OPTIONS PLAYBOOK.**™

By now, your head must be so full of option-related knowledge you probably need a bigger hat. Hopefully, you're also well on your way to making smarter trades.

If your mental hard-drive isn't quite full, check out my blog in the Learning Center on TradeKing.com. I'm constantly updating it with information that you'll find useful when placing your trades. And don't forget to refer back to this playbook while considering which strategy to run.

Now, in parting, I'd like to leave you with one simple wish:

May all the options you buy expire in-the-money, and all the ones you sell expire out-of-the-money.

Happy Trading,

Brian Overby